Mometrix
TEST PREPARATION

CPA Regulation

Exam Secrets Study Guide

I0889390

DEAR FUTURE EXAM SUCCESS STORY

First of all, **THANK YOU** for purchasing Mometrix study materials!

Second, congratulations! You are one of the few determined test-takers who are committed to doing whatever it takes to excel on your exam. **You have come to the right place.** We developed these study materials with one goal in mind: to deliver you the information you need in a format that's concise and easy to use.

In addition to optimizing your guide for the content of the test, we've outlined our recommended steps for breaking down the preparation process into small, attainable goals so you can make sure you stay on track.

We've also analyzed the entire test-taking process, identifying the most common pitfalls and showing how you can overcome them and be ready for any curveball the test throws you.

Standardized testing is one of the biggest obstacles on your road to success, which only increases the importance of doing well in the high-pressure, high-stakes environment of test day. Your results on this test could have a significant impact on your future, and this guide provides the information and practical advice to help you achieve your full potential on test day.

Your success is our success

We would love to hear from you! If you would like to share the story of your exam success or if you have any questions or comments in regard to our products, please contact us at **800-673-8175** or **support@mometrix.com**.

Thanks again for your business and we wish you continued success!

Sincerely,
The Mometrix Test Preparation Team

Need more help? Check out our flashcards at:
http://MometrixFlashcards.com/CPA

Written and edited by the Mometrix Exam Secrets Test Prep Team
Printed in the United States of America

TABLE OF CONTENTS

Introduction

Thank you for purchasing this resource! You have made the choice to prepare yourself for a test that could have a huge impact on your future, and this guide is designed to help you be fully ready for test day. Obviously, it's important to have a solid understanding of the test material, but you also need to be prepared for the unique environment and stressors of the test, so that you can perform to the best of your abilities.

For this purpose, the first section that appears in this guide is the **Secret Keys**. We've devoted countless hours to meticulously researching what works and what doesn't, and we've boiled down our findings to the five most impactful steps you can take to improve your performance on the test. We start at the beginning with study planning and move through the preparation process, all the way to the testing strategies that will help you get the most out of what you know when you're finally sitting in front of the test.

We recommend that you start preparing for your test as far in advance as possible. However, if you've bought this guide as a last-minute study resource and only have a few days before your test, we recommend that you skip over the first two Secret Keys since they address a long-term study plan.

If you struggle with **test anxiety**, we strongly encourage you to check out our recommendations for how you can overcome it. Test anxiety is a formidable foe, but it can be beaten, and we want to make sure you have the tools you need to defeat it.

Secret Key #1 – Plan Big, Study Small

There's a lot riding on your performance. If you want to ace this test, you're going to need to keep your skills sharp and the material fresh in your mind. You need a plan that lets you review everything you need to know while still fitting in your schedule. We'll break this strategy down into three categories.

Information Organization

Start with the information you already have: the official test outline. From this, you can make a complete list of all the concepts you need to cover before the test. Organize these concepts into groups that can be studied together, and create a list of any related vocabulary you need to learn so you can brush up on any difficult terms. You'll want to keep this vocabulary list handy once you actually start studying since you may need to add to it along the way.

Time Management

Once you have your set of study concepts, decide how to spread them out over the time you have left before the test. Break your study plan into small, clear goals so you have a manageable task for each day and know exactly what you're doing. Then just focus on one small step at a time. When you manage your time this way, you don't need to spend hours at a time studying. Studying a small block of content for a short period each day helps you retain information better and avoid stressing over how much you have left to do. You can relax knowing that you have a plan to cover everything in time. In order for this strategy to be effective though, you have to start studying early and stick to your schedule. Avoid the exhaustion and futility that comes from last-minute cramming!

Study Environment

The environment you study in has a big impact on your learning. Studying in a coffee shop, while probably more enjoyable, is not likely to be as fruitful as studying in a quiet room. It's important to keep distractions to a minimum. You're only planning to study for a short block of time, so make the most of it. Don't pause to check your phone or get up to find a snack. It's also important to **avoid multitasking**. Research has consistently shown that multitasking will make your studying dramatically less effective. Your study area should also be comfortable and well-lit so you don't have the distraction of straining your eyes or sitting on an uncomfortable chair.

The time of day you study is also important. You want to be rested and alert. Don't wait until just before bedtime. Study when you'll be most likely to comprehend and remember. Even better, if you know what time of day your test will be, set that time aside for study. That way your brain will be used to working on that subject at that specific time and you'll have a better chance of recalling information.

Finally, it can be helpful to team up with others who are studying for the same test. Your actual studying should be done in as isolated an environment as possible, but the work of organizing the information and setting up the study plan can be divided up. In between study sessions, you can discuss with your teammates the concepts that you're all studying and quiz each other on the details. Just be sure that your teammates are as serious about the test as you are. If you find that your study time is being replaced with social time, you might need to find a new team.

Secret Key #2 – Make Your Studying Count

You're devoting a lot of time and effort to preparing for this test, so you want to be absolutely certain it will pay off. This means doing more than just reading the content and hoping you can remember it on test day. It's important to make every minute of study count. There are two main areas you can focus on to make your studying count.

Retention

It doesn't matter how much time you study if you can't remember the material. You need to make sure you are retaining the concepts. To check your retention of the information you're learning, try recalling it at later times with minimal prompting. Try carrying around flashcards and glance at one or two from time to time or ask a friend who's also studying for the test to quiz you.

To enhance your retention, look for ways to put the information into practice so that you can apply it rather than simply recalling it. If you're using the information in practical ways, it will be much easier to remember. Similarly, it helps to solidify a concept in your mind if you're not only reading it to yourself but also explaining it to someone else. Ask a friend to let you teach them about a concept you're a little shaky on (or speak aloud to an imaginary audience if necessary). As you try to summarize, define, give examples, and answer your friend's questions, you'll understand the concepts better and they will stay with you longer. Finally, step back for a big picture view and ask yourself how each piece of information fits with the whole subject. When you link the different concepts together and see them working together as a whole, it's easier to remember the individual components.

Finally, practice showing your work on any multi-step problems, even if you're just studying. Writing out each step you take to solve a problem will help solidify the process in your mind, and you'll be more likely to remember it during the test.

Modality

Modality simply refers to the means or method by which you study. Choosing a study modality that fits your own individual learning style is crucial. No two people learn best in exactly the same way, so it's important to know your strengths and use them to your advantage.

For example, if you learn best by visualization, focus on visualizing a concept in your mind and draw an image or a diagram. Try color-coding your notes, illustrating them, or creating symbols that will trigger your mind to recall a learned concept. If you learn best by hearing or discussing information, find a study partner who learns the same way or read aloud to yourself. Think about how to put the information in your own words. Imagine that you are giving a lecture on the topic and record yourself so you can listen to it later.

For any learning style, flashcards can be helpful. Organize the information so you can take advantage of spare moments to review. Underline key words or phrases. Use different colors for different categories. Mnemonic devices (such as creating a short list in which every item starts with the same letter) can also help with retention. Find what works best for you and use it to store the information in your mind most effectively and easily.

Secret Key #3 – Practice the Right Way

Your success on test day depends not only on how many hours you put into preparing, but also on whether you prepared the right way. It's good to check along the way to see if your studying is paying off. One of the most effective ways to do this is by taking practice tests to evaluate your progress. Practice tests are useful because they show exactly where you need to improve. Every time you take a practice test, pay special attention to these three groups of questions:

- The questions you got wrong
- The questions you had to guess on, even if you guessed right
- The questions you found difficult or slow to work through

This will show you exactly what your weak areas are, and where you need to devote more study time. Ask yourself why each of these questions gave you trouble. Was it because you didn't understand the material? Was it because you didn't remember the vocabulary? Do you need more repetitions on this type of question to build speed and confidence? Dig into those questions and figure out how you can strengthen your weak areas as you go back to review the material.

Additionally, many practice tests have a section explaining the answer choices. It can be tempting to read the explanation and think that you now have a good understanding of the concept. However, an explanation likely only covers part of the question's broader context. Even if the explanation makes perfect sense, **go back and investigate** every concept related to the question until you're positive you have a thorough understanding.

As you go along, keep in mind that the practice test is just that: practice. Memorizing these questions and answers will not be very helpful on the actual test because it is unlikely to have any of the same exact questions. If you only know the right answers to the sample questions, you won't be prepared for the real thing. **Study the concepts** until you understand them fully, and then you'll be able to answer any question that shows up on the test.

It's important to wait on the practice tests until you're ready. If you take a test on your first day of study, you may be overwhelmed by the amount of material covered and how much you need to learn. Work up to it gradually.

On test day, you'll need to be prepared for answering questions, managing your time, and using the test-taking strategies you've learned. It's a lot to balance, like a mental marathon that will have a big impact on your future. Like training for a marathon, you'll need to start slowly and work your way up. When test day arrives, you'll be ready.

Start with the strategies you've read in the first two Secret Keys—plan your course and study in the way that works best for you. If you have time, consider using multiple study resources to get different approaches to the same concepts. It can be helpful to see difficult concepts from more than one angle. Then find a good source for practice tests. Many times, the test website will suggest potential study resources or provide sample tests.

Practice Test Strategy

If you're able to find at least three practice tests, we recommend this strategy:

Untimed and Open-Book Practice

Take the first test with no time constraints and with your notes and study guide handy. Take your time and focus on applying the strategies you've learned.

Timed and Open-Book Practice

Take the second practice test open-book as well, but set a timer and practice pacing yourself to finish in time.

Timed and Closed-Book Practice

Take any other practice tests as if it were test day. Set a timer and put away your study materials. Sit at a table or desk in a quiet room, imagine yourself at the testing center, and answer questions as quickly and accurately as possible.

Keep repeating timed and closed-book tests on a regular basis until you run out of practice tests or it's time for the actual test. Your mind will be ready for the schedule and stress of test day, and you'll be able to focus on recalling the material you've learned.

Secret Key #4 – Pace Yourself

Once you're fully prepared for the material on the test, your biggest challenge on test day will be managing your time. Just knowing that the clock is ticking can make you panic even if you have plenty of time left. Work on pacing yourself so you can build confidence against the time constraints of the exam. Pacing is a difficult skill to master, especially in a high-pressure environment, so **practice is vital**.

Set time expectations for your pace based on how much time is available. For example, if a section has 60 questions and the time limit is 30 minutes, you know you have to average 30 seconds or less per question in order to answer them all. Although 30 seconds is the hard limit, set 25 seconds per question as your goal, so you reserve extra time to spend on harder questions. When you budget extra time for the harder questions, you no longer have any reason to stress when those questions take longer to answer.

Don't let this time expectation distract you from working through the test at a calm, steady pace, but keep it in mind so you don't spend too much time on any one question. Recognize that taking extra time on one question you don't understand may keep you from answering two that you do understand later in the test. If your time limit for a question is up and you're still not sure of the answer, mark it and move on, and come back to it later if the time and the test format allow. If the testing format doesn't allow you to return to earlier questions, just make an educated guess; then put it out of your mind and move on.

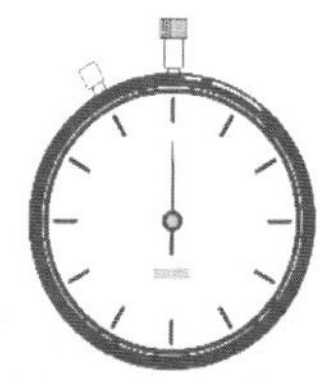

On the easier questions, be careful not to rush. It may seem wise to hurry through them so you have more time for the challenging ones, but it's not worth missing one if you know the concept and just didn't take the time to read the question fully. Work efficiently but make sure you understand the question and have looked at all of the answer choices, since more than one may seem right at first.

Even if you're paying attention to the time, you may find yourself a little behind at some point. You should speed up to get back on track, but do so wisely. Don't panic; just take a few seconds less on each question until you're caught up. Don't guess without thinking, but do look through the answer choices and eliminate any you know are wrong. If you can get down to two choices, it is often worthwhile to guess from those. Once you've chosen an answer, move on and don't dwell on any that you skipped or had to hurry through. If a question was taking too long, chances are it was one of the harder ones, so you weren't as likely to get it right anyway.

On the other hand, if you find yourself getting ahead of schedule, it may be beneficial to slow down a little. The more quickly you work, the more likely you are to make a careless mistake that will affect your score. You've budgeted time for each question, so don't be afraid to spend that time. Practice an efficient but careful pace to get the most out of the time you have.

Secret Key #5 – Have a Plan for Guessing

When you're taking the test, you may find yourself stuck on a question. Some of the answer choices seem better than others, but you don't see the one answer choice that is obviously correct. What do you do?

The scenario described above is very common, yet most test takers have not effectively prepared for it. Developing and practicing a plan for guessing may be one of the single most effective uses of your time as you get ready for the exam.

In developing your plan for guessing, there are three questions to address:

- When should you start the guessing process?
- How should you narrow down the choices?
- Which answer should you choose?

When to Start the Guessing Process

Unless your plan for guessing is to select C every time (which, despite its merits, is not what we recommend), you need to leave yourself enough time to apply your answer elimination strategies. Since you have a limited amount of time for each question, that means that if you're going to give yourself the best shot at guessing correctly, you have to decide quickly whether or not you will guess.

Of course, the best-case scenario is that you don't have to guess at all, so first, see if you can answer the question based on your knowledge of the subject and basic reasoning skills. Focus on the key words in the question and try to jog your memory of related topics. Give yourself a chance to bring the knowledge to mind, but once you realize that you don't have (or you can't access) the knowledge you need to answer the question, it's time to start the guessing process.

It's almost always better to start the guessing process too early than too late. It only takes a few seconds to remember something and answer the question from knowledge. Carefully eliminating wrong answer choices takes longer. Plus, going through the process of eliminating answer choices can actually help jog your memory.

Summary: Start the guessing process as soon as you decide that you can't answer the question based on your knowledge.

How to Narrow Down the Choices

The next chapter in this book (**Test-Taking Strategies**) includes a wide range of strategies for how to approach questions and how to look for answer choices to eliminate. You will definitely want to read those carefully, practice them, and figure out which ones work best for you. Here though, we're going to address a mindset rather than a particular strategy.

Your odds of guessing an answer correctly depend on how many options you are choosing from.

Number of options left	5	4	3	2	1
Odds of guessing correctly	20%	25%	33%	50%	100%

You can see from this chart just how valuable it is to be able to eliminate incorrect answers and make an educated guess, but there are two things that many test takers do that cause them to miss out on the benefits of guessing:

- Accidentally eliminating the correct answer
- Selecting an answer based on an impression

We'll look at the first one here, and the second one in the next section.

To avoid accidentally eliminating the correct answer, we recommend a thought exercise called **the $5 challenge**. In this challenge, you only eliminate an answer choice from contention if you are willing to bet $5 on it being wrong. Why $5? Five dollars is a small but not insignificant amount of money. It's an amount you could afford to lose but wouldn't want to throw away. And while losing $5 once might not hurt too much, doing it twenty times will set you back $100. In the same way, each small decision you make—eliminating a choice here, guessing on a question there—won't by itself impact your score very much, but when you put them all together, they can make a big difference. By holding each answer choice elimination decision to a higher standard, you can reduce the risk of accidentally eliminating the correct answer.

The $5 challenge can also be applied in a positive sense: If you are willing to bet $5 that an answer choice *is* correct, go ahead and mark it as correct.

Summary: Only eliminate an answer choice if you are willing to bet $5 that it is wrong.

Which Answer to Choose

You're taking the test. You've run into a hard question and decided you'll have to guess. You've eliminated all the answer choices you're willing to bet $5 on. Now you have to pick an answer. Why do we even need to talk about this? Why can't you just pick whichever one you feel like when the time comes?

The answer to these questions is that if you don't come into the test with a plan, you'll rely on your impression to select an answer choice, and if you do that, you risk falling into a trap. The test writers know that everyone who takes their test will be guessing on some of the questions, so they intentionally write wrong answer choices to seem plausible. You still have to pick an answer though, and if the wrong answer choices are designed to look right, how can you ever be sure that you're not falling for their trap? The best solution we've found to this dilemma is to take the decision out of your hands entirely. Here is the process we recommend:

Once you've eliminated any choices that you are confident (willing to bet $5) are wrong, select the first remaining choice as your answer.

Whether you choose to select the first remaining choice, the second, or the last, the important thing is that you use some preselected standard. Using this approach guarantees that you will not be enticed into selecting an answer choice that looks right, because you are not basing your decision on how the answer choices look.

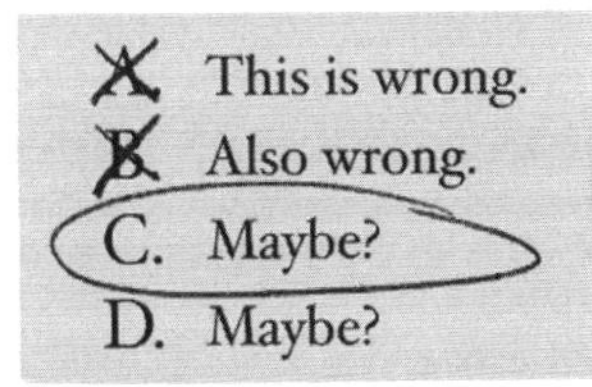

This is not meant to make you question your knowledge. Instead, it is to help you recognize the difference between your knowledge and your impressions. There's a huge difference between thinking an answer is right because of what you know, and thinking an answer is right because it looks or sounds like it should be right.

Summary: To ensure that your selection is appropriately random, make a predetermined selection from among all answer choices you have not eliminated.

Test-Taking Strategies

This section contains a list of test-taking strategies that you may find helpful as you work through the test. By taking what you know and applying logical thought, you can maximize your chances of answering any question correctly!

It is very important to realize that every question is different and every person is different: no single strategy will work on every question, and no single strategy will work for every person. That's why we've included all of them here, so you can try them out and determine which ones work best for different types of questions and which ones work best for you.

Question Strategies

☑ Read Carefully

Read the question and the answer choices carefully. Don't miss the question because you misread the terms. You have plenty of time to read each question thoroughly and make sure you understand what is being asked. Yet a happy medium must be attained, so don't waste too much time. You must read carefully and efficiently.

☑ Contextual Clues

Look for contextual clues. If the question includes a word you are not familiar with, look at the immediate context for some indication of what the word might mean. Contextual clues can often give you all the information you need to decipher the meaning of an unfamiliar word. Even if you can't determine the meaning, you may be able to narrow down the possibilities enough to make a solid guess at the answer to the question.

☑ Prefixes

If you're having trouble with a word in the question or answer choices, try dissecting it. Take advantage of every clue that the word might include. Prefixes can be a huge help. Usually, they allow you to determine a basic meaning. *Pre-* means before, *post-* means after, *pro-* is positive, *de-* is negative. From prefixes, you can get an idea of the general meaning of the word and try to put it into context.

☑ Hedge Words

Watch out for critical hedge words, such as *likely, may, can, often, almost, mostly, usually, generally, rarely,* and *sometimes.* Question writers insert these hedge phrases to cover every possibility. Often an answer choice will be wrong simply because it leaves no room for exception. Be on guard for answer choices that have definitive words such as *exactly* and *always.*

☑ Switchback Words

Stay alert for *switchbacks.* These are the words and phrases frequently used to alert you to shifts in thought. The most common switchback words are *but, although,* and *however.* Others include *nevertheless, on the other hand, even though, while, in spite of, despite,* and *regardless of.* Switchback words are important to catch because they can change the direction of the question or an answer choice.

⊘ Face Value

When in doubt, use common sense. Accept the situation in the problem at face value. Don't read too much into it. These problems will not require you to make wild assumptions. If you have to go beyond creativity and warp time or space in order to have an answer choice fit the question, then you should move on and consider the other answer choices. These are normal problems rooted in reality. The applicable relationship or explanation may not be readily apparent, but it is there for you to figure out. Use your common sense to interpret anything that isn't clear.

Answer Choice Strategies

⊘ Answer Selection

The most thorough way to pick an answer choice is to identify and eliminate wrong answers until only one is left, then confirm it is the correct answer. Sometimes an answer choice may immediately seem right, but be careful. The test writers will usually put more than one reasonable answer choice on each question, so take a second to read all of them and make sure that the other choices are not equally obvious. As long as you have time left, it is better to read every answer choice than to pick the first one that looks right without checking the others.

⊘ Answer Choice Families

An answer choice family consists of two (in rare cases, three) answer choices that are very similar in construction and cannot all be true at the same time. If you see two answer choices that are direct opposites or parallels, one of them is usually the correct answer. For instance, if one answer choice says that quantity *x* increases and another either says that quantity *x* decreases (opposite) or says that quantity *y* increases (parallel), then those answer choices would fall into the same family. An answer choice that doesn't match the construction of the answer choice family is more likely to be incorrect. Most questions will not have answer choice families, but when they do appear, you should be prepared to recognize them.

⊘ Eliminate Answers

Eliminate answer choices as soon as you realize they are wrong, but make sure you consider all possibilities. If you are eliminating answer choices and realize that the last one you are left with is also wrong, don't panic. Start over and consider each choice again. There may be something you missed the first time that you will realize on the second pass.

⊘ Avoid Fact Traps

Don't be distracted by an answer choice that is factually true but doesn't answer the question. You are looking for the choice that answers the question. Stay focused on what the question is asking for so you don't accidentally pick an answer that is true but incorrect. Always go back to the question and make sure the answer choice you've selected actually answers the question and is not merely a true statement.

⊘ Extreme Statements

In general, you should avoid answers that put forth extreme actions as standard practice or proclaim controversial ideas as established fact. An answer choice that states the "process should be used in certain situations, if..." is much more likely to be correct than one that states the "process should be discontinued completely." The first is a calm rational statement and doesn't even make a definitive, uncompromising stance, using a hedge word *if* to provide wiggle room, whereas the second choice is far more extreme.

⊘ Benchmark

As you read through the answer choices and you come across one that seems to answer the question well, mentally select that answer choice. This is not your final answer, but it's the one that will help you evaluate the other answer choices. The one that you selected is your benchmark or standard for judging each of the other answer choices. Every other answer choice must be compared to your benchmark. That choice is correct until proven otherwise by another answer choice beating it. If you find a better answer, then that one becomes your new benchmark. Once you've decided that no other choice answers the question as well as your benchmark, you have your final answer.

⊘ Predict the Answer

Before you even start looking at the answer choices, it is often best to try to predict the answer. When you come up with the answer on your own, it is easier to avoid distractions and traps because you will know exactly what to look for. The right answer choice is unlikely to be word-for-word what you came up with, but it should be a close match. Even if you are confident that you have the right answer, you should still take the time to read each option before moving on.

General Strategies

⊘ Tough Questions

If you are stumped on a problem or it appears too hard or too difficult, don't waste time. Move on! Remember though, if you can quickly check for obviously incorrect answer choices, your chances of guessing correctly are greatly improved. Before you completely give up, at least try to knock out a couple of possible answers. Eliminate what you can and then guess at the remaining answer choices before moving on.

⊘ Check Your Work

Since you will probably not know every term listed and the answer to every question, it is important that you get credit for the ones that you do know. Don't miss any questions through careless mistakes. If at all possible, try to take a second to look back over your answer selection and make sure you've selected the correct answer choice and haven't made a costly careless mistake (such as marking an answer choice that you didn't mean to mark). This quick double check should more than pay for itself in caught mistakes for the time it costs.

⊘ Pace Yourself

It's easy to be overwhelmed when you're looking at a page full of questions; your mind is confused and full of random thoughts, and the clock is ticking down faster than you would like. Calm down and maintain the pace that you have set for yourself. Especially as you get down to the last few minutes of the test, don't let the small numbers on the clock make you panic. As long as you are on track by monitoring your pace, you are guaranteed to have time for each question.

⊘ Don't Rush

It is very easy to make errors when you are in a hurry. Maintaining a fast pace in answering questions is pointless if it makes you miss questions that you would have gotten right otherwise. Test writers like to include distracting information and wrong answers that seem right. Taking a little extra time to avoid careless mistakes can make all the difference in your test score. Find a pace that allows you to be confident in the answers that you select.

✓ Keep Moving

Panicking will not help you pass the test, so do your best to stay calm and keep moving. Taking deep breaths and going through the answer elimination steps you practiced can help to break through a stress barrier and keep your pace.

Final Notes

The combination of a solid foundation of content knowledge and the confidence that comes from practicing your plan for applying that knowledge is the key to maximizing your performance on test day. As your foundation of content knowledge is built up and strengthened, you'll find that the strategies included in this chapter become more and more effective in helping you quickly sift through the distractions and traps of the test to isolate the correct answer.

Now that you're preparing to move forward into the test content chapters of this book, be sure to keep your goal in mind. As you read, think about how you will be able to apply this information on the test. If you've already seen sample questions for the test and you have an idea of the question format and style, try to come up with questions of your own that you can answer based on what you're reading. This will give you valuable practice applying your knowledge in the same ways you can expect to on test day.

Good luck and good studying!

Ethics, Professional, and Legal Responsibilities

Code of Professional Conduct

The Code of Professional Conduct for CPAs is based on ethics and its authority is derived from the bylaws of the AICPA. It is specific as to what is permissible for CPAs and applies to all AICPA members. CPAs need a code of professional conduct due to the need and desire to control actions and behavior of the members for the good of the profession and society. It is also needed to enable CPAs to gain public confidence in the quality of their service. It is imperative for CPAs to maintain a high level of integrity. The code does have similarities to other professions, such as its prohibition of discreditable acts and requirement of competence. A difference between the CPA code and other professions' required ethics is the issue of independence. The profession of public accounting has deemed it essential to promulgate the code and to establish a mechanism for enforcing observance of the code, since a distinguishing mark of a profession is its acceptance of responsibility to the public.Code compliance mainly relies upon the AICPA members' understanding of the code and their actions taken voluntarily. Once this is taken into consideration, code compliance may secondarily rely on peer reinforcement, disciplinary proceedings (CPAs may receive admonishment, up to two years of suspension, or AICPA expulsion, or acquittal), and the opinion of the public.

The Code of Professional Conduct for CPAs (Code) includes the following sections:

- Principles (not enforceable) – The ideal, philosophical foundations for the framework.
- Rules (enforceable) – Minimum standards, actual rules.

The Code has Interpretations (not enforceable) of the Rules and Ethical Rulings (not enforceable), which are published explanations and answers to questions. The AICPA Code of Professional Conduct states that a CPA shall not disclose any confidential information obtained in the course of a professional engagement except with the consent of the client. This rule precludes responding to a CPA-shareholder of the client corporation. However, if an AICPA member is thinking of selling his firm, he may allow the purchasing CPA to examine confidential client information without the client's explicit permission. In this situation, the CPAs should sign a confidentiality agreement. A CPA may discuss a client's confidential information with the CPA's lawyer or in court when facing the possibility of litigation. It is discreditable for a CPA to use false advertisement to gain clients.

Principles

The Principles of the Code of Professional Conduct are made up of the following sections:

- Responsibilities – Moral and professional judgment should be exemplified in all actions.
- Public Interest – Members should maintain consideration that the profession has a responsibility to the public.
- Integrity – All actions should be conducted with independence, objectivity, and due care to maintain the public's confidence in the profession.
- Objectivity and Independence – AICPA members must maintain independence in both fact and appearance for attestation engagements; members must remain objective in their professional activities.
- Due Care – Members should maintain care and competence in all professional areas.

- Scope and Nature of Services – Members should adhere to the code's guidelines in regard to internal quality control and in assessing the nature and scope of professional engagements.

Independence

Users of financial statements expect an unbiased viewpoint. Independence is essential to this profession, and it should be both in appearance and in fact:

- In appearance: How the auditor appears to outsiders. Independence in appearance will help maintain public confidence in the profession.
- In fact: The auditor must actually maintain an attitude of independence throughout engagement.

CPAs have motivations other than the code, such as legal liability and professionalism, to remain independent. SEC rules on independence include that the auditor cannot function in role of management, audit own work, or serve as client advocate. Additionally, there are restrictions on what auditors can do regarding consulting services, partner rotations, and employment relationships (e.g., a former audit team member might not be allowed to later work for a client company).

Treasury Department Circular 230

Treasury Department Circular 230 provides rules governing those who prepare tax returns or give tax advice (attorneys, CPAs, enrolled agents, and others) as before the Internal Revenue Service (IRS). The publication contains a number of prohibitions and requirements. It prohibits tax preparers from: (1) taking frivolous positions on tax returns, (2) charging fees for preparing original returns dependent upon the position's outcome, (3) charging an "unconscionable fee" to represent a client, (4) representing separate clients who would have conflicting interests, (5) soliciting business fraudulently, and other things.It requires tax preparers (1) to return clients' tax records, (2) to sign all prepared tax returns, (3) to give their clients copies of tax returns, (4) to notify clients of any known errors (whether committed by the client or the preparer) involving the return, (5) to submit records to the IRS punctually, and other things.

AICPA's SSTS

The AICPA's Statements on Standards for Tax Services (SSTS) provide a general framework of ethics for the tax profession. It contains statements concerning the following:

- tax return positions (any positions the preparer advised the taxpayer to take, or concluded to be appropriate, should be based on their realistic possibility);
- answers to questions on returns (tax preparers must make a reasonable effort to answer all questions on a tax return, with certain conditions specifying when answers are unnecessary);
- procedural aspects of preparing returns (e.g., the tax preparer does not need to verify third-party work, and the preparer ought to review prior year returns);
- the use of estimates (the preparer may reasonably rely on taxpayer estimates);
- departure from a position previously concluded in an administrate court or hearing;
- knowledge of error in return preparation (the preparer should notify the taxpayer and seek to retain a professional relationship, but is not obligated to notify the IRS);
- knowledge of error in administrative proceedings; and
- the form and content of advice to taxpayers (the preparer may give oral advice, though written is recommended).

Procedural Duties When Preparing Returns

According to the AICPA Statements on Standards for Tax Services (SSTS), a tax professional may take a taxpayer's claims, estimates, and other information on good faith without being required to confirm such data. However, this does not permit naivete on the tax professional's part; he ought to inquire further if information appears incorrect or has uneasy implications. Further, he should have knowledge of his clients' prior years' returns and of other clients' returns, should those clients be relevant to the first client. And if there are any conditional statements included in the tax return (e.g., if a deduction can be taken off so long as some condition is fulfilled), then it is the tax professional's duty to inquire into his client's fulfillment of such a condition.

IRC of 1986

The Internal Revenue Code (IRC), also known as the Internal Revenue Code of 1986, comprises the sum of federal tax law in the USA. It is topically organized and exhaustively covers all federally-related taxes, including income tax, payroll taxes, estate taxes, gift taxes, and excise taxes. The Internal Revenue Service (IRS) implements and enforces the regulations stipulated in the IRC.

Licensing and Disciplinary Systems for Tax Regulation

Among the licensing and disciplinary systems governing tax professionals, there are a number of different levels. There are state boards of accountancy, which set state standards for licensing and disciplinary measures, including punishments for violation of standards. There is the American Institution of Certified Public Accountants (AICPA), in addition to state CPA societies, which require compliance concerning ethics with a code of conduct. There is the Internal Revenue Service (IRS), which can execute both civil and criminal penalties for violations. There is the Securities and Exchange Commission (SEC), which can also enforce such civil and criminal penalties. And there is the Sarbanes-Oxley Act of 2002, which set much stricter regulations in overseeing accountant-company relationships.

State Boards of Accountancy

Licensing for taxation is determined according to state boards, not federally. Each state has different requirements pertaining to education, experience, and residency. Similarly, disciplinary measures are also determined on a state level, according to individual state boards, with some overlap, pertaining to transgressions of criminal activity and other misconduct, whether within or outside of the tax professional's accounting performance. The state boards vary their penalties, but the penalties involve either the revocation of one's license, the suspension of one's license, a fine, a reprimand, probation, or courses in continuing professional education (CPE).

Regulatory Agencies

The two main regulatory agencies who can monitor and control the behavior of tax professionals are the Internal Revenue Service (IRS) and the Securities and Exchange Commission (SEC). Both of these can issue civil and criminal penalties against transgressing tax professionals. Specifically, the IRS can enforce fines (as determined according to a civil court), prohibit accountants from practicing before the IRS anymore, and charge fraudulent tax preparers with up to three years' imprisonment and a $100,000 fine. The SEC may suspend or prevent accountants from practicing before the SEC and issue civil fines of up to $100,000. Further, the SEC's criminal penalties were augmented with the Sarbanes-Oxley Act: violators of SEC regulations can receive seven years' imprisonment or fines up to $1,000,000 for failing to maintain corporate audit paperwork.

Requirements of the SEC Governing Public Accountants

The requirements of the SEC over public accountants are contained in the SEC Rules of Practice. In particular, Rule 102(e) enables the SEC to take action against any public accountants who lack either the competence to properly fulfill their profession's standards or the ethical character to do so, and against those who have participated in any violations of federal securities laws or assisted others in doing the same. In addition, the SEC has regulations governing "improper professional conduct," which is generally considered to be something worse than negligence but less bad than professional recklessness.

Duties and Responsibilities of Tax Professionals

Tax professionals have a number of legal duties and responsibilities designed to hold them ethically accountable for their tax work. But not among these duties is the obligation to verify all information provided by the taxpayer. However, if the tax professional comes across information which helps him to realize that there is some error (whether of omission or commission) on the tax report, then he is obligated to inform the taxpayer and give advice on how to remedy the error, if possible. Otherwise, the tax professional's job is to ensure that the taxpayer is taxed as little as he legally needs to be. Furthermore, tax professionals are required to retain documentation of their clients' tax returns for several years, due to statutes of limitations on tax misstatements and fraud.

Tax Professionals' Common Law Duties to Clients

Tax professionals bear an obligation towards clients for contractual provisions, negligence, and fraud. Contractually, a tax professional ought to execute all of the expressed and implied duties in any contract he has with his client, with penalties imposed on him for any material breaches of contract. The tax professional is also duty-bound to refrain from negligence, according to a standard of reasonable care, with the guilt for a professional's negligence being reduced if an amount of client negligence contributed to the error (contributory negligence). And professionals are also obligated not to commit either actual fraud (fraud with the intent to deceive) or constructive fraud (fraud built upon extreme negligence), or else pay punitive damages.

Tax Professionals' Civil Duties to Third Parties Under Common Law

Tax professionals can have various liabilities to third parties under common law. Any third-party beneficiary of a contract (i.e., a party to whom the client seeks to pass on benefits gained in the contract—a party who may enforce contractual provisions despite not strictly being a contractual party) can receive damages for material breach of contract. Any negligence which leads to third-party harm brings guilt upon the professional if he knew or ought to have known of the effects his work would have had on the third parties. However, with fraud (active or constructive), guilt for third-party damages is incurred regardless of the tax professional's awareness of the third parties' dependence on his work.

Common Law Treatment of Negligence, Fraud, and Constructive Fraud

Under common law, there can be liability to clients based on negligence. Negligence is the failure of the auditor to conduct the audit with "due care." It is covered by malpractice insurance. To prove negligence, the following needs to be shown:

- The CPA had the responsibility to exhibit the competence expected in the profession.
- The CPA did not fulfill his responsibility as expected from his profession.
- There is a causal relationship between the plaintiff's damages and the CPA's error.

Under common law, the CPA cannot be held liable due to an honest judgment error. He must have exhibited negligence in his actions. There is also a common law liability to the client for fraud, constructive fraud, or gross negligence. Under common law, a CPA's liability for fraud, constructive fraud, or gross negligence is determined by the following factors: scienter, actual damages, misrepresentation of the CPA's expert opinion or of material fact, and the injured party's reasonable or justifiable reliance. For fraud, gross negligence, and constructive fraud:

- Punitive damages can be added to actual damages.
- The plaintiff does not have to prove privity of contract.
- The CPA cannot use the client's contributory negligence as a defense.

Tax Professionals' Liability for Negligence

If a tax professional does not exercise due care in his dealings with his clients, then he could be liable for negligence to them. The tax professional needs to act in accord with a standard of reasonable care, which permits certain errors of inaccuracy and judgment, but only those which do not constitute negligence. If a client's negligence in providing or checking information contributes in some way to the professional's negligence in overlooking some error, then the client's contributory negligence mitigates the liability of the professional. And while clients can receive damages for the harm caused or the loss that would have been avoided due to professional negligence, there are generally no punitive damages required of negligent professionals.

Accountants' Liability to Third Parties

There are a number of federal-law regulations governing an accountat's duties to third parties. These are all contained in the Securities Act of 1933, the Securities Exchange Act of 1934, the Private Securities Litigation Reform Act of 1995, and the Sarbanes-Oxley Act of 2002.

- The 1933 act seeks to hold accountants responsible for materially false or misleading statements in financial statements.
- The 1934 act requires the issuance of a company's annual report (the Form 10-K) and holds accountants as civilly liable for any material misstatements or omissions in any annual reports.
- The 1995 act amends the acts of 1933 and 1934, seeking to increase the likelihood that public accountants detect and disclose corporate fraud. The accountant is required to inform management, the audit committee, and the board of directors of any entity in which he detects material error fraud.
- The 2002 act led to the creation of the Public Company Accounting Oversight Board (PCAOB), which oversees the relations between public accountants and their client companies. It emphasizes auditor independence in both fact and appearance by prohibiting auditors to engage in certain non-auditing services with client companies, and otherwise taking steps to minimize conflicts of interest.

CPA-client relationship

There is no accountant-client privilege granted by common law; if this privilege exists, it must be created by statute. Although there are a few states with this privilege, the federal government does not acknowledge this privilege. If a client commits an illegal act, the CPA may notify other parties with the following:

- Successor auditor disclosures
- Disclosures in response to subpoena
- Disclosures through change of auditors in the Form 8-K
- For companies receiving governmental assistance financially, the CPA can provide disclosure to the funding agency

Auditors cannot delegate an audit because the work is considered to be personal services and there is a contract.

Securities Act of 1933

The Securities Act of 1933 was a landmark piece of legislation that provided government regulation over the initial issuance of securities, addressed registration and disclosure, and intended to give possible investors complete disclosure pertaining to securities to enable them to make a well-informed decision. This act prohibits any security registration statement from including any false material information or leaving out any material information. Under this act, registered securities purchasers and third parties may sue. The act requires that companies provide a prospectus and registration statement to the SEC for review. The act applies to both noncorporate and corporate security issuers. The SEC does not assess the securities' value; they only require companies to fully disclose all pertinent information. This act does contain antifraud provisions as well. A requirement of a private action to recover damages for violation of the registration requirements of the Securities Act of 1933 is that the plaintiff has acquired the securities in question. Criminal liability exists under the act, even when the transactions or securities are exempt. The act has created more protection for public company whistleblowers. Civil liability exists under the act by securities purchasers bringing private actions under the act.

Private Securities Litigation Reform Act

If the auditor does not comply with the act, the SEC may enforce civil liability. CPAs auditing companies subject to the act must develop audit procedures to discover material illegal acts, discover material related-party transactions, and assess the client's capability to carry on as a going concern. If an auditor discovers illegal actions, he must notify either the board of directors or the audit committee. This act has been instrumental in decreasing the number of lawsuits against CPAs. This act has limited pointless class action lawsuits. For example, it has instituted a "safe harbor" from legal liability for the preparation of financial forecasts and financial projections. This act altered rules on several and joint liability, making it so that defendants' liability is in proportion to their extent of responsibility. There is an exception if the defendant intentionally caused damage.

Privileged Communications and Confidentiality

The AICPA Code of Professional Conduct states that a CPA shall not disclose any confidential information obtained in the course of a professional engagement except with the consent of the client. This rule precludes responding to a CPA-shareholder of the client corporation. However, if an AICPA member is thinking of selling his firm, he may allow the purchasing CPA to examine confidential client information without the client's explicit permission. In this situation, the CPAs should sign a confidentiality agreement. A CPA may discuss a client's confidential information with the CPA's lawyer or in court when facing the possibility of litigation.

Business Law

Principal Disclosure in an Agency Relationship

Principal disclosure in an agency relationship:

- Undisclosed principal: Identity and existence is kept secret to a third party. The third party may hold either the agent or principal liable in the case of an undisclosed principal. The agent is considered a contract party.
- Partially disclosed principal: Third parties are not informed of the identity of the principal; they are only informed of the existence of the principal
- Disclosed principal: Third parties are informed of the principal's identity when an agent acts on behalf of the principal. In cases of an agent without authority entering a contract in the name of a disclosed principal when the principal has not ratified the contract, the third party and principal are not liable to each other.

Principal-Agent Relationship and Agency Coupled with an Interest

The Principal-Agent Relationship is a fiduciary relationship in which the agent is granted some independent discretion and may take action for the principal in business transactions or bind the principal in a contract with a third party. An agency can be entered into for any legal purpose, but it is a consensual relationship rather than a contractual relationship. It is not necessary for consideration to be given to the agent from the principal. Contractual capacity is not a requirement of an agent. Since an agent can enter into a contract on the principal's behalf, a principal should have contractual capacity. Should a principal not have contractual capacity, contracts may be voided by the principal but not by the third party. Power of attorney and broker are examples of agency relationships. In an agency relationship, a principal is liable as a party to a lawful contract made by an agent on his behalf and for torts committed by the agent acting in his actual or apparent authority or subsequently ratified by the principal. Should a third party seek to recover from a principal, the third party is required to prove the existence of the agency relationship and that the agent was behaving in accordance with his apparent or actual authority, or that the agent's behavior was ratified by the principal. An agency coupled with an interest is an agency relationship in which the agent is given an estate or interest in the subject of the agency; an agency coupled with an interest cannot be canceled by the principal.

Agent's Remedies and Principal's Remedies

Remedies are comprised of those existing in cases of torts or contract breaches. An agent may opt to bring a damages suit due to contract breach, or an act of tort, or a counterclaim, if the principal sues the agent. Additionally, an agent can get back compensation for unpaid past performance and future damages. The agent cannot make the principal continue to employ the agent. Principal's remedies available in an agency relationship are as follows:

- Indemnification – The principal is permitted to be paid damages from the agent if the principal is forced to pay damages to an injured party for an agent's torts or if the agent disregards the instructions from the principal and the principal incurs losses as a result.
- Constructive trust – The courts will enforce a constructive trust on property that the agent receives when the agent has used his position in conflict with the principal and the property is treated as held for the principal's benefit.
- Avoidance – If the agent fails to abide by the agency agreement, any transactions entered into by the agent may be voided by the principal

- Principals are permitted to recover from the agent should the agent commit a contract breach, fiduciary duty breach, or tort. In these cases, the principal may also elect to discontinue the agency relationship.

Entering into an Agency Relationship

An agency relationship can be entered into by agreement, operation of law, estoppel, or ratification. Agency by agreement is accomplished by mutual consent of both the principal and agent; this agreement can be either expressly written or oral, or implied by the parties' behavior. Agency can be formed as a result of estoppel: if a principal causes a third party to believe that another person was his agent, a principal can possibly be estopped to refute the existence of an agency. An agency relationship can be formed as a result of implied or express ratification. Ratification is associated with a previous time in which an agent acted without the principal's authorization; after a supposed agent acts as the principal's agent, the principal's consent can be granted.

Termination of an Agency Relationship

An agency relationshiop can be terminated by operation of law or by the parties:

- Operation of law – A change of circumstances can cause agency termination. If the agency subject matter is damaged, an agency can be terminated. An agency is terminated if either the principal or agent dies or becomes incompetent; an agency coupled with an interest is not terminated immediately.
- The parties – The parties may terminate an agency relationship by fulfilling the agency purpose, a lapse of time, and mutual agreement. An agent may relinquish his agent position; a principal may choose to cancel the agent's authority.

If an agency relationship is terminated by one of the parties, the agency will continue until the terminating party informs the other party. Third parties should also be informed of the agency termination; constructive notice, such as a newspaper ad or a sign, should be given.

Agent's Authority

An agent has the following authority:

- Implied authority: May be determined based on the principal's behavior; may be determined due to customs or traditions.
- Ratification: Principal's confirmation that his permission is granted for a previously unauthorized transaction, act, or contract. The complete transaction must be ratified. The principal should be given all material relevant information regarding the transaction. One requirement is that the principal should have had legal capacity at the time of the performance of the act and at the time of the act's ratification. Ratification can be either express or implied.
- Express actual authority: Can be granted either in writing or verbally.
- Powers in emergency: Should an unexpected emergency present itself to the agency, and if the agent cannot contact the principal, the agent has the authority to act in the best interest of the principal.
- Actual authority: Granted by the principal either implicitly or explicitly.
- Apparent authority: The principal behaves in a manner giving the appearance that the agent has the principal's authorization.

Duties of Principal to Agent

Some duties are listed in the agency agreement. The agency relationship also assumes further duties:

- Duty to reimburse: The principal should cover any liabilities acquired by an agent as he is carrying out his duties.
- Duty to compensate: The principal does not have a responsibility to compensate an agent who has not fulfilled his duties properly. Assuming an agent fulfills his duties, a principal must compensate the agent the agreed-upon amount; if there is no specific compensation amount determined, the principal must pay the agent's expenses, losses, and reasonable compensation for the agent's duties performed.
- Duty to cooperate: The principal should never stop an agent from fulfilling his duties and should help the agent accordingly.
- Duty to grant safe working environment
- Rights of agent: reimbursement, compensation, and safe working conditions to work in

Duties of Agent to Principal

The foundation of the agency relationship is trust. The agent has the following duties to the principal:

- Duty of performance: Should an agent not perform his duty appropriately, the agent may be held liable for the tort of negligence or breach of contract.
- Duty of obedience: In an emergency situation, an agent who cannot make contact with his principal may deviate.
- Duty of notification: An agent should inform the principal of any relevant material information associated with the agency's subject matter.
- Duty of accounting: An agent should disclose any money or property transactions that the agent has handled on the principal's behalf; an agent should not commingle his funds with the funds of the principal.
- Duty of loyalty: During and following an agency termination, an agent is not permitted to divulge any confidential information learned during his employment.

Contracts

A contract is any agreement between two or more parties legally obligating them to perform or refrain from some action. Contracts can be explicit (formed by verbal or written articulation) or implicit (formed by actions and surrounding circumstances). For each condition of the contract, the one obligated to perform the term is the promisor, and the one with the right to receive the benefits of such performance is the promisee. Contracts are bilateral if two parties are each obligated to fulfill terms which they have promised to execute, but they are unilateral if only one party has promised such. In the case of unilateral contracts, one party will still have some action to perform, which will then obligate the other party to pay—but the one party is not obligated to perform that action in the first place (e.g. finding a lost wallet to get a lost-and-found reward). Some contracts are illegal, in which case they are not enforceable. Illegal contracts include agreements violating public policies, services performed by parties without a license when a license is required, contracts to commit illegal actions, and not pursuing legal action for consideration.

Definiteness and Communication of Contract and Contract Term

All of the major terms must be stated with reasonable definiteness in the offer (or, if the offeror directs, in the offeree's acceptance). Sometimes, courts are willing to supply a missing term when the parties have clearly manifested intent to form a contract. The offer must be communicated to the offeree. An offer can be terminated in the following methods by either termination by action of the parties or termination by operation of law:

- The offeror usually can revoke the offer (even if he has promised to keep it open) by express repudiation or by performance of acts that are inconsistent with the offer and that are made known to the offeree.
- Revocation must be communicated to the offeree (or the offeree's agent) before the offeree accepts. A revocation becomes effective when the offeree or offeree's agent actually receives it.
- An offer made to the general public can be revoked in the same manner the offer was originally communicated.

Consideration

Consideration is a promise or act that one party will offer to encourage another party to accept and reach an accord. One important factor is that the consideration must be the result of a bargain; past consideration cannot be used to arrange a new contract since it is not bargained for. For consideration to be valid, it must be sufficient legally. If modifying an existing contract, both parties involved need to have new consideration for the contract to be legally binding. However, under the Uniform Commercial Code (UCC), consideration is not required for a contract involving the sale of goods; as long as both parties are in good faith, the contract may be modified either in writing or orally. Preexisting legal duty does not qualify as appropriate consideration. As a general rule, moral obligation does not qualify as appropriate consideration. Promissory estoppel is the doctrine that prevents a party from acting in a certain way because the first party promised not to, and the second party relied on that promise and acted upon it. Promissory estoppel is recognized as a consideration substitute and causes the promise to be enforceable. In a contract, either both parties are bound by obligation, or neither party is bound by obligation.

Remedies

Remedies can include specific performance, release, reformation, monetary damages, restitution, waiver, arbitration, injunction, and rescission. For reformation to take place, the courts require unmistakable proof. Specific performance is required only when monetary damages will not be adequate; compensatory damages may also be pursued. Specific performance cannot be required for contracts regarding personal services. As a general rule, punitive damages are not permitted in contract law. Monetary damages are awarded to compensate the injured party by making up for the contract not being performed. Compensatory damages should be equal to the loss caused by the breach in contract; compensatory damages are the most frequently used remedy in contract law. Some contracts contain a liquidated damages clause, which states the damages amount should a contract breach take place.

Quasi-Contracts

A quasi-contract is a term used in civil law to refer to an act of a person, permitted by law, by which he obligates himself towards another, or by which another binds himself to him, without any agreement between them. By the Civil Code of Louisiana, quasi-contracts are defined to be "the lawful and purely voluntary acts of a man, from which there results any obligation whatever to a third person, and sometime a reciprocal obligation between the parties." In contracts, it is the consent of the contracting parties which produces the obligation; in quasi-contracts, no consent is required, and the obligation arises from the law or natural equity, on the facts of the case. These acts are called quasi-contracts because, without being contracts, they bind the parties just as contracts do.

BILATERAL CONTRACTS

A bilateral contract is an agreement in which the parties exchange promises for each to do something in the future. Suppose that Susan Seller promises to sell her house to Bob Buyer, and Buyer promises to pay Seller $100,000 for it. This is distinct from a "unilateral contract," in which there is a promise to pay if the other party chooses to do something, e.g. "I'll pay you $1,000 if you'll stop smoking." Unilateral contracts include obligations which are activated should some party fulfill a condition, even though that party is not himself obligated to fulfill that condition.

EXPRESS CONTRACT AND IMPLIED CONTRACT

An express contract is a contract in which all elements are specifically stated (offer, acceptance, consideration), and the terms are stated, as compared to an "implied" contract, in which the existence of the contract is assumed by the circumstances. A contract may be both written and express, but may not be both oral and implied. An implied contract is an agreement which is found to exist based on the circumstances, such that denying a contract would be unfair or results in unjust enrichment for one of the parties. An implied contract is distinguished from an "express contract."

CONTRACT REQUIREMENTS

Intention is required for an offer. For a contract to be made, an agreement must be reached. The parties involved in a contract are the offeror (who makes an offer) and the offeree (to whom the offer is made). If, through the process of offer and acceptance, an agreement is reached, and the other elements are present (consideration, capacity, legality), a valid contract is formed. A contract must contain reasonably definite terms. Generally, a contract must include, either expressed or implied in the contract, the following terms: identification of the parties, identification of the contract's subject matter (including quantity), the consideration to be paid, and the time of performance.

IRREVOCABLE OFFERS, REJECTION OF OFFER BY OFFEREE, AND COUNTEROFFER BY OFFEREE

Irrevocable offers can occur either with an option contract or with detrimental reliance. An option contract is a promise that an offer will be held available for a specified period of time. An option contract is an additional contract that takes away the offeror's power to revoke the offer for the period of time specified. If no time is particularly specified, a reasonable time is then implicit for the offer's duration. If a party dies or is incompetent, however, that does not generally terminate an option contract. Factors involved in detrimental reliance include promissory estoppel and unilateral contracts. Promissory estoppel is the doctrine which prevents an offeror from revoking his offer when the offeree justifiably relies on it to his or her detriment. The offer may be rejected by the offeree through words or conduct that evince his intent not to accept the offer. If an offeree has subsequent attempts to accept the offer, they will be construed as a new offer, making the offeree a new offeror. Rejection of an offer is effective only when the offeror actually receives it; simply inquiring about an offer is not rejecting it. A counteroffer is an offeree's attempt to include different terms. It involves a rejection of the original offer and the presentation of a new offer. The mirror image rule requires the acceptance to match the offer exactly.

UNAUTHORIZED MEANS OF ACCEPTANCE, REJECTION AND ACCEPTANCE, LEGALITY, AND STATUTE OF LIMITATIONS

An unauthorized means of acceptance occurs when there is a mode of communication which is prohibited by the offeror. In such a case, the offer is officially valid when it is received. Otherwise, it is considered effective when sent, so long as acceptance is timely (i.e. made before the offer is terminated). An offeree might send a rejection but then, after changing his mind, send an acceptance (or vice versa). In these cases, the first message to be received by the offeror is determinative of whether the contract is formed. Illegal contracts cannot be enforced. They are any contracts which are in violation of public policies, which require services to be performed by unlicensed party if the service requires a license, or which do not pursue legal action for consideration. The statute of limitations for breaches of contract is different by state. If a lawsuit for breach of contract is not initiated with the designated time period, a lawsuit is forbidden.

Void or Voidable Contracts and Contract Performance

If a contract has any of the following elements, it may be considered void or voidable: fraud, duress, mistakes, unintentional misrepresentations, incompetency, noncompliance with the statute of frauds, undue influence, adhesion contracts, or unconscionable contracts. Fraud includes the following factors: *scienter*, misrepresentation of a material fact, and the injured party's reasonable reliance. Should fraud exist, the injured party may disaffirm the agreement and sue for damages, or affirm the contract and sue for damages. Fraud may exist in the contract execution (causing a void contract) or in the agreement negotiations (causing a voidable contract). In cases of duress or undue influence, an agreement can be voided. In the case of an unintentional misrepresentation, the injured party may cancel the contract. If both parties make a mistake regarding the subject matter's material characteristics, the agreement becomes voidable for either party. If only one party makes a mistake, the contract is usually not voidable, unless it relates to a bid computation. The tender of performance is considered to be an offer to perform. A party's duty to perform may possibly be dependent upon a condition to be performed prior to or following a duty stated in the contract.

Formation of Contracts

Contracts are ordinarily formed through the offering process. An offer is a promise or commitment to do or refrain from doing some specified thing in the future. Offers may be either oral or written, and the offeror must intend to be bound by the offer. The offeror's intent is determined by what a reasonable person in the offeree's position would conclude the offeror's words and actions meant. Offers made in obvious anger, jest, or undue excitement do not qualify. What appears to be an offer may not be sufficient to form the basis of a contract. It is important to recognize what does not constitute an offer. For an offer to be valid, it must be definite and specific as to the terms to be agreed upon; it must also be sufficiently communicated by the offeror to the offeree. Nonoffers include: expressions of opinion, statements of intention, preliminary negotiations, advertisements, catalogues, price lists, and circulars. Auctions represent a special situation. Agreements to agree to a material term of a contract at some future date may be enforced if the parties clearly intend to be bound.

Offers Under Uniform Commercial Code

It may be difficult to determine when a contract becomes effective. It is permitted for contracts to contain open terms; that is, a contract can still be formed if some terms remain open if the parties definitely intended to develop a contract. The contract may not specify open payment terms; if this is the case, it is assumed that when the buyer obtains possession of the goods, the payment will be due. Delivery terms of a contract may be open as well. If there is no designated delivery location, it is assumed that the goods should be delivered at the place of business or home of the seller. If there is never a delivery time designated during the time that the contract is in place, the terminating party is required to give sufficient notice to the other party. The exact amount of goods involved in the transaction is unsure in an output or requirements contract. The lack of consideration in these agreements is acceptable.

Acceptance Under Uniform Commercial Code

If a communication of acceptance method has not been designated, any reasonable communication method may be used; as soon as the communication of acceptance is sent, it is considered to be effective. Sometimes an offeree will inform the offeror of his intention of acceptance; however, he will want to alter the current contract terms. If the seller and buyer are merchants, the altered terms are included in the contract, unless any of the following are true: a) The altered terms alter the offer materially; b) the offeror informs the offeree of the offeror's lack of satisfaction with the new terms; or c) the offer explicitly states that acceptance can only occur with its original terms. If either the seller or buyer (or both) are not merchants, the offeree's communication of the proposal of new terms is considered to be an effective acceptance of the agreed-upon terms. In cases of a unilateral contract offeree failing to inform the offeror of the offeree's beginning performance, the offeror is permitted to interpret the offer as if it lapsed prior to his receiving acceptance. When a seller promises to ship or ships conforming goods, an offer to buy the goods is accepted. Should a seller ship nonconforming goods, the seller is considered to accept and breach the contract. However, should a seller inform the buyer that he is shipping nonconforming goods, the shipment is considered to be a counteroffer. If the buyer accepts the nonconforming goods, the contract is formed.

Contract Formation in Electronic Age

A signature on a faxed document is legally binding. When an acceptance is faxed but is not received in a timely fashion, it will not be considered effective until it is received. Additionally, clicking on a computer screen constitutes a valid acceptance of a contractual offer. Electronic signatures are also considered to be valid. As a general rule, shrink wrap agreements tend to be enforceable when the customer was given sufficient time to review the terms of the license including the liability limitations and forum choice. Under both common law and UCC, offers, rejections, revocations, and counteroffers are valid when received. The purpose of the Uniform Electronic Transaction Act (UETA) is to support the enforceability of electronic contracts. Thus, the presumption is that e-contracts are valid. UETA applies automatically whenever the parties agree to use e-commerce. An E-contract requires a "record." This means 1) it is stored in an electronic or other medium and 2) it is retrievable. Any electronic symbol intended as a signature is enforceable.

Contract Performance

Contract performance is the most common way for a contract to be discharged, referring to the basic completion of all parties' contractual obligations. Performance can be either complete (where the contractual terms are exactly or nearly exactly fulfilled) or substantial (where performance is incomplete, but only minorly so, and done in good faith). Substantial performance warrants a lesser but proportionate contractual fulfillment by the other party. There can be various conditions to performance which surround and modify the contractual obligations of the parties involved. A condition precedent is any uncertain event which needs to occur before any performance duty arises. A condition subsequent is an uncertain event which, if it occurs, dissolves an already-existing contractual duty for a party to perform. And a condition concurrent refers to the parties' obligation to discharge their contractual obligations simultaneously (or near simultaneously). If a party attempts or offers to perform its side of the contract, then it has made a tender. If the other party refuses to accept a tender, the tender-offering party could be relieved of its contractual duty and could sue the other party for breach of contract.

Contract Assignment

A contract assignment occurs when a contract right is transferred by one of the original parties for the contract (the assignor) to a different party (the assignee). An assignment is not permitted if the right is personally related to the promise or would compromise a confidential relationship if assigned, or if the duty of the promisor would be materially altered. In addition to these conditions, assignments can be plainly prohibited in the terms of the contract.

Contract Dismissal

Contract dismissal can be done by a contract breach, an anticipatory breach, an agreement, or by performance.

Dismissal by agreement:

- Rescission - The parties choose to cancel the contract. Both parties are returned to their pre-contract positions. Rescission is for contracts that are executory on both sides. The consideration that supports the rescission agreement is that both parties give up their rights to enforce the original contract.
- Novation - This is a separate contract where the original parties and a new third party agree that the third party will substitute for one of the original parties. It must be signed by all of the original parties and the new party. The substituted party is completely discharged.
- Accord and satisfaction - Parties agree to different performance to discharge the original contract (For example, deliver my order to my home instead of my business.) The accord is the different performance agreed to by the parties. The satisfaction is the performance of the different obligation (delivery to the house). The satisfaction of the accord discharges the original obligation.

Disaffirming a contract: Should either party cause a breach in a contract, the injured party may disaffirm the contract. However, as opposed to common law rescission, under the Uniform Commercial Code, disaffirming the contract does not discharge a damages claim.

Anticipatory repudiation: If either party in a contract informs the other party that he does not intend to perform, the hurt party has the following options: a.) choose another remedy, such as getting another contract or suing; b.) discontinue his own performance; c.) wait for the other party to either take back the repudiation or perform according to the contract.

Legal Capacity for Contract Purposes

A contract is considered void or voidable if either one or both parties lack the legal capacity to participate. If an insane party participates in the forming of a contract, the contract is considered void; if the contract was entered into prior to the insane party becoming insane, the contract will possibly be voidable by the insane party. A minor may enter into a contract, but the contract is considered voidable by the minor. Until a reasonable time after reaching the age of legal capacity, a minor may opt to disaffirm a contract. Minors are liable for the reasonable value of necessities such as food, clothing, and shelter under the quasi-contract doctrine. Once a minor reaches 18, he may ratify the contract expressly or by conduct (i.e. continue to enjoy the benefits of the contract).

Auctions

In an auction, the bid is considered to be the offer. Until the auctioneer declares the sale to be completed, the bidder may withdraw his bid, or offer. Auctions are considered to be "with reserve," unless stated otherwise. For an auction "with reserve," until the auctioneer has declared the sale to be completed, the auctioneer may retract the goods. In an auction "without reserve," unless there is no bid made, the goods may not be retracted.

Employer-Employee Relationship

For an employer-employee relationship, the courts will examine the circumstances to determine whether or not such a relationship has been established. It is important to determine whether a relationship is an employment relationship or agency relationship for purposes of social security, taxes, unemployment, workers compensation, etc. The following are evidence of an employment relationship:

- The employee is paid on a regular basis instead of on results.
- The employer provides the employee with the necessary supplies and equipment to perform the employee's duties.
- The employee performs his duties at the employer's place of business.
- The employee is directly supervised by either the employer or his representative.

Employer-Independent Contractor Relationship

Regarding an employer-independent contractor relationships, an employer cannot be bound in a contract with a third party by an independent contractor. Typically, an independent contractor is paid upon completion of a project. The independent contractor will normally work with his own supplies and equipment to complete his responsibilities.

Respondeat Superior Doctrine

The *respondeat superior* doctrine teaches that the principal (employer) is responsible for the actions of his agent/employee in the "course of employment."

- Employee/agent negligence liability - A principal/employer is not permitted to disclaim contractual liability for an agent/employee's torts. A significant deviation from the principal/employer's place of business and the agent/employee's responsibilities is considered to be outside the scope of employment/agency. Should a principal/employer have the right to manage a "borrowed" employee, the principal/employer is held liable for the borrowed employee's torts.
- Liability for employee/agent's intentional torts - Should an employee/agent commit a tort at the employer's direction, although the employee/agent was not aware that the act was wrong, the principal/employer and agent/employee are liable.
- Independent contractor's tort liability – Employers will not be held liable for an independent contractor injuring a third party by an intentional tort; however, both the employer and independent contractor will have strict liability enforced if the independent contractor is participating in dangerous actions.
- Crime liability – Should an agent/employee commit a crime without the principal/employer's involvement, the agent/employee is held liable for his actions; the principal/employer is not held liable.

Insurance

Insurance is intended for risk transferal and allocation. It will cover an uncontrollable, unexpected contingency. If this contingency is realized, someone will suffer a significant financial loss. The individual states are responsible for regulating the insurance industry. Most states require that insurance policies be evidenced in writing; however, the Statute of Frauds does not require writing, since the insurance contract may be within the one-year rule. An insurance policy is a type of contract in which the policy holder must have an insurable interest in the insurance subject matter; insurance policies, like common law contracts, are required to have legality, consideration, agreement, and capacity. The insurance policy becomes effective upon the insurer's notification of acceptance of the insurance application to the insured party. Insurance unilateral contracts are cases when the insurer commits to cover insured losses if the insured party prepays the insurance premiums. As a general rule, insurance policies will not cover the insured's intentional acts, such as setting fire to a building to receive the insurance proceeds. Self-insurance is also an option to protect against losses, in which money will be set aside to assist should one experience a loss. The insurer may opt to void an insurance policy in cases of the insured's material misrepresentation, policy breaches of warranty, or concealment on the part of the insured.

Uniform Commercial Code

The Uniform Commercial Code (UCC) does not deal with real property or services. Article 2 of the UCC discusses sales of goods contracts; lease contracts are addressed in Article 2A. According to Article 4, banks provide a means to transfer and collect commercial paper. Articles 3 and 5 state that payments for goods can be handled with the use of commercial paper. Article 7 addresses goods being stored and shipped. Article 9 discusses secured transactions being used in cases of buyers being granted credit. Article 2 addresses goods, or personal property; it does not pertain to real or intangible property or services. These include crops and other similar items attached to land, as well as minerals and natural resources that are removed from land. Computer software and food service contracts are considered to be sales of goods contracts.

Common Law vs. Uniform Commercial Code

Under the UCC, the sale of goods requires a signed written offer (referred to as a firm offer) from a merchant, ensuring that the offer will be open for a designated period of time, no greater than three months. This firm offer does not require consideration. Differences between options and firm offers include the following:

- the firm offer rule is not valid under common law
- options are valid under both common law and the UCC
- options are not restricted to the time period of three months
- options require consideration.

Unless otherwise noted in the offer, under the UCC, acceptance is considered valid if sent via a reasonable method. Under the UCC, unequivocal acceptance of an offer for the sale of goods is not required. An acceptance can be given by either a seller's promise to ship or by the seller shipping the goods.

Contracts for Sale or Return and Sale on Approval

In sale or return contracts, the goods are delivered for the primary purpose of resale; an example would be the sale of baseball cards. The title and risk of loss shift from the seller to the buyer when the buyer takes possession of the goods at the completion of the sale. The buyer is responsible for any expense and risk of return. If the goods are not returned within a designated time period, the sale is considered to be final; if the buyer ships the goods back to the seller, the risk of loss is on the buyer during shipment. As long as the goods are in the buyer's possession, the buyer's creditors have access to the goods unless the interest of the seller is posted and filed. In sale on approval the goods are delivered for the primary purpose of **use**; an example would be the sale of equipment. Title and risk of loss do not pass from the seller to the buyer until the buyer accepts the goods. In a sale on approval contract, conforming goods may even be returned; the sale of the goods is not final until the buyer accepts or approves the sale. The goods are not accessible by creditors until the buyer accepts the sale.

Warranty of Title and Express Warranties

A warranty of title is a warranty that the seller possesses the right to sell the goods without anyone else having a claim to the goods. It is present in a normal sale-of-goods contract. There is a breach of warranty of title if the seller does not have this right; the seller is then liable to the buyer. This warranty provides the understanding that the seller has clear title to the goods and the transfer of the title from the seller to the buyer is right. In a contract for the sale of goods, the warranty of title may be disclaimed, left out, or modified. Should the sale transaction be made and no assurances are made to the seller, the warranty of title is left out. Express warranties are statements that are either verbal or written pertaining to the state of the goods. These stated characteristics provide the foundation of the bargaining for the goods. There are no specific words that must be used in the development of an express warranty. Unless made by professionals, information of value and opinion are not considered to be an express warranty. There is a distinction between a seller's express warranty and a seller's exaggerations.

Negotiable Instruments

Negotiable instruments can be categorized as promises or orders, depending on the designated time of payment. Orders to pay include checks and drafts. Drafts involve the following parties: payee, drawer, and drawee. Drafts include bank drafts, banker's acceptance, and trade acceptance. Drafts may be used for fund transfers, account collections, and property financing. Checks include traveler's checks and cashier's checks.

Promises to pay include certificates of deposit (CDs) and promissory notes. Promissory notes involve the following parties: payee and maker. Promissory notes include collateral notes, installment notes, and mortgage notes. Promissory notes may be used for credit substitutes in order to obtain goods, services, or loans.

Secured Transactions

Secured transactions are loans or other credit-related transactions where the creditor has a claim to some security of the borrower in case the borrower cannot repay the creditor. Since secured transactions give creditors more assurance that their loans will be appropriately repaid, it encourages them to lend at lower interest rates, thereby increasing the transfer of capital and facilitating economic growth.

Documents of Title and Title Transfer

Documents of title are any documents related to the ownership of a piece of property, including any transportation the property might undergo as it is transferred from seller to buyer. These documents include bills of lading, dock warrants and receipts, warehouse receipts, orders for the delivery of goods, and others. Title cannot pass from the seller to the buyer until the goods exist and are identified. Unless otherwise noted in the contract, the title will pass from the seller to the buyer upon the seller's physical delivery of the goods. For destination contracts, the title passes from the seller to the buyer upon the delivery of the goods to the specified destination. If the parties noted in the contract that the seller must deliver title documentation to the buyer, the title is passed upon delivery of the title documentation.

Risk of Loss

Risk of loss cannot move from the seller to the buyer until the goods exist and have been identified. If the contract does not note when risk of loss shifts from the seller to the buyer, it automatically shifts when the goods are in existence and have been identified. The buyer and seller may decide when and how the risk of loss will pass from the seller to the buyer:

- The parties may decide to ship the goods. If the contract does not specify any shipping terms, the seller holds conforming goods for the buyer; the seller will inform the buyer when the goods are ready for the buyer to take delivery of them.
- If the goods are shipped FOB (free on board) shipping point, risk of loss and title will pass from the seller to the buyer upon delivery of the goods to the carrier; the buyer is responsible for the shipping costs.

- If the goods are shipped FOB destination, the title and risk of loss will pass from the seller to the buyer when the seller has the goods at a specified destination; the seller is responsible for the shipping costs.
- If goods are shipped COD (cash on delivery), the carrier cannot release the goods to the buyer until the buyer pays for the goods. Unless otherwise noted in the contract, the buyer is not permitted to inspect the goods prior to paying for them.

Rights and Remedies of Creditor and Surety or Guarantor

Should the debtor not fulfill his obligation to the creditor, the creditor has the right to seek fulfillment of the obligation from the surety. The creditor's rights include expecting fulfillment of the debtor's obligation from the debtor. Should the debtor fail to do so, the creditor may take action against the debtor. In the event of the debtor owing numerous debts to the creditor, the debtor may submit payments and specify the specific debt to which the payment should be applied. If the surety pays the debt, the surety is entitled to the debtor's reimbursement or to subrogation. Prior to the surety's agreement to being a surety, the creditor is required to disclose pertinent information regarding material risks. Upon the time for debt payment, exoneration may be an option, if the creditor is insistent upon immediate performance of the surety.

Property Rights of Secured Creditors

Suppose a debtor bought a washing machine from Sears for $500, agreed to make payments, and gave Sears a secured interest in the washing machine. If the debtor fails to make payments, Sears may repossess the washing machine within 45 days of the filing date. If the debtor seeks to retain the washing machine, the debtor may re-affirm the debt. Re-affirming the debt means that the debt will not be discharged in bankruptcy. The debtor will still be responsible for the debt. It would be unwise to re-affirm debts because the debtor could not afford his debts to begin with or he wouldn't be in bankruptcy. He will likely be unable to pay this debt in the future.

Liens Between Debtor and Creditor

Types of liens that may exist between a debtor and creditor:

- Lien: a party's right to take action to fulfill an obligation
- Artisan lien: lien permitting an artisan to retain possession of a piece of work until it has been paid for
- Innkeeper lien: permits a hotel to maintain possession of the baggage of a guest until the hotel bills have been paid
- Judgment lien: A lien on the property of a debtor resulting from a court's judgment
- Mechanic's lien: lien to secure payment for work and materials in erecting or repairing a building or other structure

Guaranty and Suretyship

Usually, contracts for both guaranty and suretyship should fulfill the specified contract factors. Guaranty or suretyship may be entered into by individuals, partnerships, or (most commonly) corporations. As a general rule, an individual partner cannot enter into a suretyship for a partnership. Participating parties include the guarantor, debtor, and creditor. A third party promises that if a debtor does not pay a debt, the third party will pay the debtor's debt.

Examples of guaranty and suretyship agreements:

- The directors of a company may agree to be a surety for a loan granted by a bank.
- A land purchaser may begin to pay the land seller's mortgage; the seller acts as a surety.

The difference between guaranty and suretyship is that the guarantor is generally secondarily liable and the surety is generally primarily liable. Contracts that are not considered to be a guaranty or suretyship are:

- Indemnity contract
- Third-party beneficiary contract

Defenses Available in Guaranty or Suretyship for Guarantor or Surety

The surety has the option of using his contractual defenses in cases of fraud, illegality of the contract, lack of consideration, the surety's incapacity, or the failure to document the suretyship contract in writing. If the creditor has acted in good faith, the surety will not be discharged from his responsibility if the primary debtor committed fraud to convince the surety to participate. The contract is voidable for the surety if the creditor gains the surety's commitment by fraud. The surety is not liable if the creditor uses fraud to gain the debtor's commitment. Typically, the debtor's defenses are options for the surety as well in the following situations: statute of limitations, breach committed by the creditor, creditor's fraudulent acts in gaining the debtor's commitment, and inability to complete performance. There are defenses available to the surety should the debtor or creditor cause material changes in the surety's commitment. The surety is released if either the debtor fulfills his obligation or the creditor takes possession of the collateral. The surety will be released from his obligation should the creditor discharge the primary debtor without the surety's permission. The surety will be released from his commitment should the debtor fulfill his obligation and the creditor does not accept the debtor's fulfillment. Personal defenses of the primary debtor are not available as the surety's defenses.

Chapter 11 Bankruptcy and Chapter 13 Bankruptcy

Chapter 11 bankruptcy was developed to assist businesses with extensive financial difficulties. It is available to partnerships, corporations, and individuals. Chapter 11 bankruptcy functions as an alternative to Chapter 7 bankruptcy and allows debtors to maintain their business assets. Courts have the option of changing a Chapter 11 business reorganization bankruptcy into a Chapter 7 bankruptcy. The SEC has very limited involvement in Chapter 11 bankruptcy proceedings. Creditors and stockholders in different classes form committees to develop a reorganization plan. Additionally, Chapter 11 business reorganization allows for a rehabilitation plan that is supervised by the bankruptcy court. Chapter 13 bankruptcy is available to people with a consistent income, secured debts of less than $1,081,400, and unsecured debts of less than $360,475. Chapter 13 bankruptcy begins upon a debtor voluntarily filing.

Chapter 7 Bankruptcy

Chapter 7 bankruptcy is also referred to as a liquidation or straight bankruptcy. It is permitted under federal law. Chapter 7 bankruptcy can be either voluntary or involuntary.

In a voluntary bankruptcy filing, the debtor is not required to be insolvent. A husband and wife may jointly file bankruptcy. Voluntary bankruptcy filing is available to individuals, partnerships, and corporations; it is not available to banks, savings and loans, and insurance companies. For voluntary bankruptcy, the debtor will file in court and will include a listing of all assets and liabilities. As soon as the debtor files for bankruptcy, the debtor is granted an immediate order of relief. In cases where a debtor has mostly consumer debts, the judicial system may refuse to grant the bankruptcy petition; should this occur, a debtor may opt to pursue Chapter 13 bankruptcy.

Creditor Order of Priority in Bankruptcy Proceedings

Creditors with priority

- Unpaid alimony/spousal support claims and child support
- Administration expenses of the bankruptcy
- Debtor's attorney
- Bankruptcy trustee
- Gap unsecured creditors
- Creditors such as the phone company, the electric company for bills that accrued between filing of petition and the discharge
- Wages, salaries, commissions earned within the 180 days prior to filing the petition, limited to $10,950 per claimant.
- Unsecured claims for contributions to employee benefit plans for services rendered within 180 days of filing the petition (e.g., an employer's contribution to health insurance premiums)
- Storage of fish and grain up to $5,400 per claimant
- Consumer deposits for purchases, leases or rentals of property or services for personal or family use, up to $2,425 per claimant
- Security deposit of tenant
- Layaway payment for goods
- Taxes

Bankruptcy Discharge

The court must determine that the debtor is honest in order to grant a bankruptcy discharge. The bankruptcy discharge grants a debtor release from all allowable debts that were not paid in bankruptcy. The following actions disallow the bankruptcy discharge of all debts:

- The debtor's noncompliance with court orders
- Inappropriate behavior during the legal proceedings, such as hiding property or falsely stating claims against the estate
- Not providing thorough details regarding any asset losses
- Inappropriate destruction of financial records
- Receiving a bankruptcy discharge during the last six years.

A bankruptcy discharge can be withdrawn should it be discovered that fraud was committed during the legal proceedings; there is a one-year limit. A bankruptcy discharge can also be rescinded should the debtor not abide by a legal court order.

Bankruptcy Alternatives, Bankruptcy Timeline, and Intended Use of Bankruptcy

Bankruptcy alternatives:

- Creditors may agree to accept less than the amount owed.
- Creditors may decide that the benefits do not outweigh the cost to pursue collection of the debt; creditors may wait it out to see if the debtor can pay the debt in the future.
- Creditors may choose to pursue payments via the legal system, such as wage garnishments.

Bankruptcy timeline:

- One year before filing:
- Insider voidable preferences

- Fraudulent transfer period
- 90 days before filing - voidable preferences
- Filing date – automatic stay
- One year after filing - discharge

Intended use of bankruptcy

- Permit insolvent debtors with integrity to give up the majority of their assets to gain relief from their debts; allows debtors to start over.
- Provide creditors with a chance to receive a portion of the debtor's assets proportionate to the debt owed to the creditor
- Bankruptcy is primarily developed from federal law.

SOX

The Sarbanes-Oxley Act of 2002 (SOX) introduced new regulations to the accounting profession and ended a sizable amount of self-regulation. This act is applicable to all public companies. It developed new federal crimes pertaining to intentional nonretention of audit workpapers. This act brought a significant focus to internal control; it requires that upper management communicate all significant internal control deficiencies to the auditors and audit committee. Additionally, the act instituted a requirement for management to recognize that it is in charge of ensuring appropriate internal controls over financial reporting and disclosing the effectiveness of its internal control. The act also compels management to comply with certain securities laws for designated reports that must be filed with the SEC. The Sarbanes-Oxley Act prohibits accounting firms that are not registered with the PCAOB from preparing or issuing audit reports on U.S. public companies and from participating in such audits. The act also provides that any non-U.S. public accounting firm that prepares or furnishes an audit report with respect to any U.S. public company is subject to the PCAOB's rules to the same extent as a U.S. public accounting firm. The board also requires that non-U.S. public accounting firms that do not issue such reports, but that play a substantial role in the preparation of the audit reports, register.

Securities Exchange Act of 1934

The Securities Exchange Act of 1934 addressed the trading of already outstanding securities; national securities exchanges must register. This act created federal regulation over the securities exchange. The provisions require the distribution of financial statements prior to or concurrent with a proxy solicitation. The SEC requires an annual report from companies. This act is designed to help diminish insider trading and fraud. Sellers and purchasers of registered securities may sue under the act. Securities issued for the purpose of financing business reorganizations, employee stock purchase plans, and the issuance of stock warrants are covered by the act. The SEC and private parties have civil remedies against violators of the act. This act extended the statute of limitations for securities fraud. The following is required under the act or the SEC's reporting requirements issued pursuant thereto:

- Reporting by issuers of securities that are actively traded over-the-counter.
- Should a corporation president be charged by the SEC with a criminal violation, a fine or prison term, or both, may be imposed.
- Section 10(b) of the Securities Exchange Act of 1934 applies to purchases and sales of securities in interstate commerce.
- If an insider sells company stock within six months of the stock purchase, the company can recover the profits.

Antifraud Provisions, Violations, Requirements for Insiders, Civil Liability, and Criminal Liability

Civil liability exists under the Securities Exchange Act of 1934 for any party controlling a security; both sellers and buyers may recover under this act. Civil liability also exists for any party providing false statements regarding material facts. Violations of the act may lead to the following:

- Suspension of securities trading
- Registration suspension
- Registration rejection

The act provides an expansive range of antifraud provisions:

- Forbids the use of any misleading methods in securities sales and purchases; this is applicable for all securities – both securities that are registered and securities not registered
- Forbids the creation of the illusion of active trading

Criminal liability exists under the act for parties providing false information on material facts deliberately; the Sarbanes-Oxley Act increased criminal liability under the act. Under the act, insiders are required to report the amount of equity securities and ownership changes within two days. Insiders are required to provide this information when the registration statement becomes effective, when the securities are registered, or in the ten days after becoming an insider.

Trade Secret, Patent, and Copyright Laws

Trade secrets laws have been implemented to protect trade secrets that may provide businesses with advantages against competitors. Patent law has been implemented to protect art, methods, machines, etc. Inventors may not obtain patents for an obvious "invention." Patents are usually in effect for twenty years after the filing of the patent application. In the United States of America, patent protection goes to the first person to invent the invention, not to the first person to file for a patent. Patent law remedies include damages, royalties, and injunctions. Copyright law has been implemented to protect original works, such as music or literature. Copyrights that have been created after 1977 are in place for the author's lifespan plus another seventy years. Works that have been published since 1988 do not need a notice of the copyright on the works. Due to the fair use doctrine, others are permitted to use works in a limited manner without being in violation of the copyright.

Debtors and Creditors Acts

- Equal Credit Opportunity Act: Ensures that all consumers are given an equal chance to obtain credit. Factors such as income, expenses, debt, and credit history are considerations for creditworthiness. Factors such as sex, color, age, marital status, race, and religion should not be considerations for creditworthiness.
- Fair Credit Billing Act: Applies to disputes about "billing errors" for "open end" credit accounts, such as credit cards, and revolving charge accounts - such as department store accounts. It does not cover installment contracts - loans or extensions of credit you repay on a fixed schedule.
- Fair Credit and Charge Card Disclosure Act: Requires disclosure by credit and charge card issuers with respect to information pertaining to interest rates and other fees which may be incurred by consumers through the use of any credit or charge card.
- Fair Debt Collection Practices Act: Offers protection from illegal and unethical debt collection tactics.

- Fair Credit Reporting Act: Designed to promote accuracy and ensure the privacy of the information used in consumer reports.
- Truth-in-Lending Act: Designed to protect consumers in credit transactions by requiring clear disclosure of key terms of the lending arrangement and all costs.

Internet Securities Offering and Antitrust Laws

- Internet Securities Offering – Predominantly used to accumulate capital by small businesses. The SEC has developed an electronic database containing corporate information; prospectuses may be posted online. Internet Securities Offerings are subject to securities laws and regulations.
- Antitrust Laws – Laws from the federal government created to promote competition, increase the efficiency of the market, and limit trade practices that are unfair. The primary antitrust laws include:
- Sherman Antitrust Act of 1890 – Prohibits monopolies in any form.
- Federal Trade Commission Act of 1914 – Established the organization that is charged with preventing competition methods that are unfair and prohibiting anything restraining trade; the FTC examines reports of boycotts, espionage, and bribery.
- Clayton Antitrust Act of 1914 – Passed as an amendment to the Sherman Antitrust Act. This act prohibited the following: horizontal mergers, price discrimination, tying arrangements, and exclusive dealerships. This act also prohibited one individual from being the director of two competing firms (known as interlocking directorates).

Mandates of Patient Protection and Affordable Care (PPACA)/Obamacare

There are two mandates in Obamacare. The **individual mandate** requires individuals to have "minimum essential coverage" or else pay a penalty on their tax return (1040) if they do not have a qualifying exemption. The **employer mandate** requires applicable large employers (ALEs)—defined as having at least 50 full-time or full-time-equivalent employees—to offer minimum essential coverage to at least 95% of their employees. For the better enforcing of these mandates, the PPACA also imposes certain reporting requirements on insurers and employers.

Reporting Requirements of PPACA/Obamacare

Obamacare imposes two forms on insurers, the 1095-B and 1094-B, and two forms on employers, the 1095-C and 1094-C.

- 1095-B: Insurers report to individuals the health coverage they had for the year.
- 1094-B: Insurers file this to transmit their Forms 1095-B to the IRS.
- 1095-C: Employers report to employees the coverage they had or were offered.
- 1094-C: Employers file this to transmit their Forms 1095-C to the IRS.

Sole Proprietorship and Regular Corporations

A sole proprietorship is an unincorporated business with only one owner. The one owner has unlimited liability and 100% of the net worth. Regular corporations are legal entities in which ownership is reflected by shares of stock. Corporation earnings are taxed at both the corporate level and at the shareholder level. Corporations are separate taxable entities. In corporations, the shareholders' personal assets are protected from any creditors' claims. Corporations have unlimited life and limited liability for shareholders. Owner, or shareholder, changes do not affect the corporation's existence. In the United States, many larger businesses choose to function as a corporation; corporations are useful in raising significant amounts of capital for the business with the use of stock ownership. In a corporation, stock shares may be freely transferred. In a corporation, the board of directors is responsible for management; the board of directors will typically appoint officers who are responsible for taking care of the business of the corporation.

Partnerships

General partnerships have at least one general partner; the partners have not designated a limited partner. General partners have unlimited joint and several liability, meaning that creditors may have access to the general partner's personal assets to pay partnership debts. Even if the general partner was not personally involved in cases of malpractice, malpractice judgments against a partnership may be satisfied by assets of all general partners. Typically, service businesses, such as medicine, accounting, or law are created as a general partnership or a limited liability partnership. In a limited liability partnership (LLP), partners are only responsible for their own individual negligence, fraud, or malpractice. Service providers, such as CPAs, lawyers, architects, and doctors, will often operate as an LLP. A limited partnership is often utilized in the acquisition of capital for activities such as the development of real estate. In a limited partnership, a limited partner's risk of loss is limited to the partner's investment of equity in the entity. Limited partners are not permitted to actively manage partnerships. Limited partnerships are often created as tax shelters. However, the tax benefits for limited partners are restricted, as they are viewed as passive investments.

Corporations

A corporation is legally distinct from its owners, the shareholders. Corporations have many similar functions as individual taxpayers, which include paying taxes, suing, and borrowing money. To incorporate, a corporate charter must be acquired in the state of incorporation. Corporations have the primary disadvantage of double taxation; their profits are taxed at the corporate level as well as at the shareholder level. The primary advantage of incorporating a business is the limited liability to the owners. Shareholders can lose up to the extent of their initial investment; shareholders are not responsible personally for corporation liabilities. Unlike sole proprietorships or partnerships, corporations have the capability of raising money by selling stock or issuing bonds, both of which are available to the general public. When stock shares are purchased, the shareholder is given a stock certificate, which lists the stock type and number of shares purchased. A corporation also has unlimited life. Should a shareholder die or sell his stock, the corporation continues to exist.

Advantages and Disadvantages of Forming Partnerships or Sole Proprietorships

A sole proprietorship is advantageous in the amount of control afforded to the owner; he is free to do entirely as he wishes with the business, including having an extremely flexible work schedule. Sole proprietorships are relatively simple and cost-effective to start up, because the fixed costs are so small. (For instance, many begin in the owner's house, or simply function online.) Lastly, it is also helpful that profits and losses from sole proprietorships can be reflected directly on the owner's personal income statement. On the other hand, since owners have full authority in a sole proprietorship, they also have full liability; their personal assets (not under the auspices of the business) are claimable for legal purposes if the owner is sued or goes into severe debt. Additionally, it can be quite burdensome to run one's own business, and when or if the business grows, it can be difficult to delegate responsibilities. Raising capital is also much more difficult for sole proprietorships. The same advantages and disadvantages exist for partnerships, except that the pros and cons are slightly different in terms of control. Each partner has less than total control, and therefore each is not burdened with the tasks of doing everything. Nevertheless, in general partnerships, each partner has unlimited liability; their personal assets are also at risk for the other partner's miscues.

Forming a Partnership and Calculating the Basis

Partners and partnerships are considered to be separate units, or entities. The majority of partnership elections for tax purposes are decided at the partnership level; this includes an accounting method, depreciation method, method of inventory, and the taxable year. Entity gains and losses types and amounts are decided at the partnership level. Earnings, credits, deductions, gains, and losses flow to the partners from the partnership for tax reporting. Organizational expenses for partnerships are handled in the same manner as corporations. Typically, there is no gain or loss recognition to either the partners or the partnership for capital contributions. Partners acquire a substituted basis in their partnership interest; when partners make property contributions, the partner acquires the adjusted basis of the contributed property as his partnership interest. The partnership takes the partner's basis in the property, or a carryover basis. A partner's interest holding period begins on the partnership interest date of acquisition; cash contributions are subject to this holding period. However, if the partner contributes property that was either a capital asset or a § 1231 asset, the partner's interest holding period will include the contributed property's holding period. The holding period of the contributing partner is included in the holding period for the partnership's contributed property.

Formation of Sole Proprietorships and Corporations

When a sole proprietorship is formed, the owner is not strictly required to formally or legally take any steps (at any level of government), but can simply start doing business. However, the locality most likely will require the owner to register his business (including the "doing business as" (DBA) name) and seek business or occupational licenses for doing business. To form a corporation, one must create a business name which is compliant with state corporation regulations, appoint directors, file the articles of incorporation and pay the filing fee, establish corporate bylaws, have the first meeting for the board of directors, issue the company's first stock certificates, and acquire the requisite licenses or permits needed to run business operations.

Dissolution and Termination of Partnerships

The dissolution of a partnersip occurs when one of the partners is no longer involved from the partnership, whether this occurs by death, resignation, or being expelled by other partners. In the case of dissolution, partners must disagree how to distribute assets or else resolve the matter in court. The termination of a partnership occurs when the business no longer operates. The partnership stays active during the dissolution process, as the partners will have an ongoing process of asset-distribution. One of the conditions which brings about termination is when, during a twelve-month period, at least 50% of the capital and profits of the partnership are sold or exchanged.

Personal Holding Company Taxes and Consent Dividends

Personal holding company (PHC) taxes were established to dissuade corporations owned by individuals in high tax brackets from protecting specific types of passive income. The PHC tax is designed to encourage corporate earnings to be distributed to shareholders. In addition to regular tax rates, PHCs are taxed an additional 15% on undistributed income for taxable years following 2002. Corporations are supposed to assess their PHC status; a six-year statute of limitations is applicable if the appropriate form is not completed. The corporation does have the option to pay dividends to lower PHC income.

To qualify as a PHC, the following two tests must be met:

- At least 60% of the corporate income is earned from passive income, such as rents and royalties or dividends and interest.
- A maximum of five people were the owners of over 50% of the outstanding stock during the last half of the tax year.

Consent dividends are a hypothetical distribution of corporate income that the shareholders will be taxed on. The consent dividend is perceived as a capital contribution, and the shareholder's stock basis goes up accordingly.

Corporation Gains and Losses

Corporations do not recognize gains or losses due to capital contributions; gross income does not include shareholder contributions as capital. Shareholders recognize no gain or loss for a transferal of property to a corporation. The corporation assumes the shareholder's basis in the transferred property. The transferred property basis is added to the shareholder's stock basis. Nonshareholder contributions are not included in a corporation's gross income; if a nonshareholder transfers property to a corporation in exchange for goods or services, the transaction is included in the gross income of the corporation and the property basis is zero. If property is depreciable to a buyer, gains are considered to be ordinary income when the property is sold to or from a shareholder owning over 50% or between corporations that are primarily owned by the same person. Issuance of stock or debt does not result in the recognition of gain or loss by a corporation. Gains are recognized upon the distribution of appreciated property to corporation shareholders. In sole proprietorships, the owner may be able to deduct losses, since all income and expenses pass to the owner. For partnerships, losses are passed through to the owners, who may be able to deduct the losses on their personal tax returns. In S corporations, losses are passed to the shareholders. For regular corporations, losses are not passed to the shareholders and do not affect them.

JOBS Act

The Jumpstart Our Business Startups Act, or JOBS Act for short, makes various exemptions from securities regulations for certain small companies, in an effort to encourage their capital funding. The law specifically was passed with reference to the phenomenon of crowdfunding, i.e., acquiring grassroots financial support via the internet. The JOBS Act consists of seven different Titles, though Titles II and III are the most prominently discussed. Title I defines a new category of stock-issuing company, called an emerging growth company (EGC), to which the Act applies. Generally, this includes all new small businesses. Title II removes the prohibition against EGCs' solicitation to the general public. However, such businesses can only receive actual investments from "accredited investors" (roughly, institutions and high-income or high-net-worth individuals). EGCs are required to file forms with the SEC regarding solicitation and are to verify that investors are accredited. Title III permits non-accredited investors to invest in EGCs, though with limits on the total capital raised and on the total amount an individual non-accredited investor can contribute. Title V changes the requirements for when companies must register with the SEC. Previously the firm needed assets exceeding $10 million and over 500 shareholders; now the issuing threshold is either 2,000 total holders, or 500 non-accredited holders.

Federal Taxation Process, Accounting, and Planning

Federal Tax Legislative Process

In the House of Representatives, tax legislation is proposed first to the House Ways and Means Committee, who then approve or disapprove a bill and pass it on for approval or disapproval by the entire House. The Senate Finance Committee performs an analogous role for the Senate. Since senators can amend bills and make them different from the bills that passed through the House, sometimes a joint committee will convene to solve any disputes between conflicting versions of the bill. If a bill is passed by congress, it is offered to the president to sign or to veto. The president can sign the bill within ten days, or the veto can be overridden by two-thirds vote of both the House and Senate, in order for the bill to become law and become part of the Internal Revenue Code (IRC).

Due Dates and Extensions for Federal Tax Returns

For corporations and partnerships, federal income tax returns are due by the fifteenth day of the third month after the close of the tax year, which works out to March 15 when operating according to a normal calendar year. For individuals, estates, and trusts, federal income tax returns are due by the fifteenth day of the fourth month after the tax year, which works out to April 15 for an ordinary calendar year. Exempt organizations have an extra month in addition (May 15). Estate tax returns are due nine months following the decedent's death, whereas gift tax returns are due when an individual's income tax is ordinarily due. If a donor dies after providing the gift, it is treated as an estate tax. Due dates which occur on holidays or weekends are not applicable; in such cases the due date is pushed to the next business day. While extensions can be sought to postpone the due date for six months (or more), the extensions apply merely to the filing of the return—not to the payment of the tax itself.

IRS Audit and Appeals Process

The IRS is authorized to inspect taxpayers' records in order to determine their tax liability. If the IRS believes there is a tax deficiency for some taxpayer, then the IRS can issue a statutory notice of deficiency; it is sometimes called a "90-day letter," since there is a 90-day period after the notice is sent before payment is requested. The taxpayer thus has 90 days to dispute the claim. Once a notice and demand for payment is issued, the taxpayer generally has 30 days to pay, unless the IRS demands immediate payment (e.g., if they believe payment will not be made in 30 days). If the taxpayer does not pay, the IRS is authorized to possess the taxpayer's property and wages until the deficiency is restored.

Audits and Statute of Limitations Regarding Tax Administration

The Treasury Department administers federal tax law. The IRS, as a part of the Treasury Department, may review questionable returns at an IRS office, by correspondence with the taxpayer, or at the taxpayer's business location. An IRS examiner may propose tax return changes for individual taxpayers. If the taxpayer does not agree with the proposed changes, he may meet with the examiner's supervisor. The taxpayer will receive a 30-day letter listing the proposed changes, along with the examination report. The taxpayer has 30 days to appeal the findings of the examiner, accept the proposed changes, or ignore the first letter and wait for a statutory notice of deficiency (90-day letter). The taxpayer is allowed 90 days to file a Tax Court petition. The assessment period ceases for 150 days following the mailing of the 90 day letter. The IRS has 3 years from an income tax return filing to assess additional tax liability against a taxpayer. For early filers, the 3 years begin on the tax return due date. For late filers, the 3 years begin on the date the return was filed. If a taxpayer leaves out a gross income amount greater than 25% of the gross income claimed on the return, the statute of limitations is six years. If a taxpayer does not file a return, or files a fraudulent return, there is no statute of limitations for tax assessments. Typically, refund claims must be filed within three years of the filing date or within two years from the tax payment date, whichever is later.

Returns Selected for Audits

The IRS has not disclosed its exhaustive criteria by which it selects returns to audit, though it does seek returns which are most likely to be in error and most likely to be in error by a significant amount. Taxpayers most likely to be audited include the following: individuals earning a high gross income, self-employed persons with sizable business deductions, businesses which deal mostly in cash, people who have previously had a tax deficiency, taxpayers with greater than normal itemized deductions for their income, taxpayers who have filed a refund claim, and others.

Audit Procedures and RAR

The IRS must discuss the audit process with the taxpayer before or during the first interview the IRS has with the taxpayer; and the interview must be suspended by the IRS if the taxpayer expresses that he wants to consult with someone who could represent him before the IRS, such as an attorney, CPA, or enrolled agent. The Revenue Agent's Report (RAR) results from the audit performed by an IRS agent, where he details the nature of the audit and the findings, including the amount of tax deficiency (or refund). Taxpayers can dispute with an agent's report through the IRS Appeals Division or the U.S. Tax Court.

Taking Disputes to Court

When a taxpayer wishes to dispute an IRS report but is ineffective in utilizing the IRS Appeals Division, he still has legal recourse. He can appeal to a court of original jurisdiction, which has four different kinds of courts: the Small Cases Division (regarding $50,000 or less), the Federal District Court, the U.S. Court of Federal Claims, and the U.S. Tax Court. There are also a number of appellate courts to which taxpayers can appeal: U.S. Courts of Appeals for geographical districts and the U.S. Court of Appeals for the Federal Circuit.

Role of Courts in Formation of Tax Law

Tax law can be dependent on the precedents made through other authoritative bodies or proclamations. This does not apply to cases from the Small Cases Division (which cannot be appealed and which do not set precedent), but other courts can create judicial law through precedent, with Federal District Courts setting precedent only for their own district. Courts of original jurisdiction are required to follow precedents established by the court of appeals of jurisdiction, and they are required to follow precedents established by the U.S. Supreme Court.

Required Disclosure of Tax Return Positions

Beginning with tax returns for the tax year 2010, the IRS requires the submission of a Schedule of Uncertain Tax Positions (UTP) as part of the tax returns for certain corporations. Corporations must disclose to the IRS each U.S. federal income tax position taken with respect to particular deductions or reserves. In 2010, it applied only to companies with assets exceeding $100 million, though the requirement dropped to $50 million for 2012 and dropped to $10 million for 2014 and beyond.

Substantiation Requirements for Taxpayer When Appealing Tax Liability

To credibly defend himself and place the burden of proof upon the IRS, a taxpayer must fulfill four conditions:

- he must substantiate items,
- he must keep satisfactory records,
- he must comply when the IRS reasonably asks for interviews and data, and
- he must have a net worth under $7 million.

If these four conditions are fulfilled, it is the IRS's burden to prove the taxpayer's tax liability.

Penalties Taxpayers Can Receive for Tax Violations

Taxpayers can be fined for failing to pay their tax obligation, though the fine is avoidable if the taxpayer's failures are reasonably caused and not due to outright neglect.

- This starts with a fine of 0.5% of the amount due per month, up to 25% maximum. This penalty then doubles upon the IRS's issuance of a notice of deficiency.
- The fine for failing to file one's tax return is 5% of the amount per month, up to 25%. If it is more than 60 days late, the minimum penalty is the lesser of $435 or 100% of the unpaid tax, for returns required to be filed on or after 1/1/2023.
- The IRS can charge a penalty concerning the accuracy of a financial statement item, generally 20% of the understated amount. This applies to particular inaccuracies arising from negligent disregard of tax regulations, substantial understatement of tax liability, or substantial overstatement or understatement of a valuation.
- The IRS charges an improper refund penalty of 20% for any refund which is claimed but not granted, if the taxpayer cannot provide reasonable support for his claim.
- The IRS can charge several other types of penalties, including criminal penalties of imprisonment and/or $100,000 maximum for individuals and $500,000 maximum for corporations, in addition to litigation fees. Criminal penalties are incurred only for willful violation of tax regulations beyond a shadow of a doubt.

Statute of Limitations for Tax Violations

The IRS has three years from an income tax return filing to assess additional tax liability against a taxpayer. For early filers, the three years begin on the tax return due date. For late filers, the three years begin on the date the return was filed. If a taxpayer leaves out a gross income amount greater than 25% of the gross income claimed on the return, the statute of limitations is six years. If a taxpayer does not file a return, or if he files a fraudulent return, there is no statute of limitations for tax assessments. Typically, refund claims must be filed within three years of the filing date or within two years from the tax payment date, whichever is later.

Accounting Periods Figured into One's Taxes

If a taxpayer keeps accurate records for his inflows and outflows, he can use a fiscal year, that is, a twelve-month period which ends on the last day of a month besides December. Otherwise, he is required to pay annual taxes according to a standard calendar year. The IRS's consent is required if the taxpayer wishes to change his accounting period.

- For individuals, taxpayers who are married and filing jointly must use the same taxpayer.
- C corporations can choose between a calendar year and a fiscal year. S corporations and personal service corporations (PSCs) are required to use calendar years unless they have good business reasons to do otherwise. Partnerships generally use the same accounting period as the partners do individually, unless (again) there is a good business reason to do otherwise.
- Estates can choose to have a calendar-year or fiscal-year accounting period, but trusts must have a calendar year.

Recognizing Revenues and Expenses

Taxpayers with annual gross receipts under $1 million may use the cash method of accounting rather than the accrual method. However, if a taxpayer must take account of inventory, then he is required to use the accrual method for recognizing sales and cost of goods sold. Corporations are almost always forbidden from utilizing the cash method of accounting, although a non-tax-shelter entity which is a qualified personal service corporation (PSC) or which has under $5 million in gross receipts may use it.

Effects of Inventory Valuation on Taxes

The Uniform Capitalization Rules (UNICAP) give regulations for the capitalization of costs (all indirect and most direct) for producing property, particularly for the production of real and tangible property which the taxpayer produces for the purpose of business transactions or investment. However, taxpayers can be exempt from the regulations over property obtained for resale if the average gross receipts over the past three years are under $10 million. The major inventory valuation that affects one's taxes is whether one accounts for inventory with LIFO or FIFO accounting. The regulations require that if a taxpayer uses LIFO for tax accounting, then he must also use it for financial accounting purposes.

Percentage-of-Completion Method for Long-Term Contracts

The percentage-of-completion method is used when accounting for long-term contracts, in which a portion of the contract price gross amount is included in each period's income as the work progresses. The percentage of completion method is used unless the transaction is eligible for the completed-contract method, which is used for home construction contracts and other particular real estate construction contracts. The percentage-of-completion method uses the following calculation in determining each period's (excluding the last accrual) revenue accrual:

> [(contract costs incurred during period/estimated total cost of the contract) * price of the contract]

All contract allocated costs during the period are deductible from revenue accrued. The final period revenue reported is the unreported contract revenue. If less than 10% of the total estimated contract costs have been incurred at the conclusion of the accounting period, the taxpayer may choose not to recognize income or costs from a contract for that tax period.

Installment Method for Reporting Gains

The installment method is applicable to gains from property sales resulting in the seller's receipt of at least one payment following the year of sale. This method does not change the gain character (such as capital or ordinary); the installment method must be used except for cases in which the taxpayer makes a negative election to report the complete gain amount during the accounting period in which it was sold. The reportable amount is calculated by the following:

[(gross profit/total contract price) * amount received in the year]

The installment method is not permitted for Internal Revenue Code Sections 1245 and 1250 depreciation recapture; gains on property held for sale during the normal course of business; and gains on stocks or securities traded on an established market.

Entity Classification Election

Entity classification election is relevant for business entities who may want to be treated as a corporation or as some other business entity depending upon how such classification would affect their obligations for federal income tax and for most states' income tax. This election can be done through the filing of the IRS Form 8832. Without submitting such a form, an entity will simply receive its default classification. Any U.S. corporations and foreign entities that can be publicly traded are not permitted to seek entity reclassification. And if any entity owned by more than one owner does not have a default classification of a corporation, its default classification is a partnership.

Considerations When Planning Taxes to Maximize Long-Term Benefits

The taxpayer should seek to balance short-term benefits and long-term costs. He might have the option of decreasing or deferring his taxes in the short term, but this should be done only if the taxes for future years will not undo the benefits of the current year's tax relief. There might be non-tax benefits associated with paying taxes at a certain time, such that deferring taxes might not be in one's best interest. There are different considerations for taxes related to different kinds of business entities. Corporations have to deal with double taxation, but can have non-taxable fringe benefit programs. Sometimes preserving the form of a tax transaction (that is, as opposed to its substance) is important for decreasing one's total tax obligations.

Actions Taken to Lower One's Tax Obligations

One can reduce taxable income by contributing one's funds to a Roth IRA, acquiring bonds whose interest is non-taxable, and obtaining employee benefits which are non-taxable instead of a pay increase, which would be taxable.

- One can defer taxes by deferring the income one receives, contributing funds to a traditional IRA, and giving appreciated business assets to a budding corporation or partnership.
- One can reduce one's tax rate by giving gifts of income-generating property to family members with a lower income and by giving gifts of appreciated property to family members with lower capital gain tax rates.
- One can avoid double taxation by having a limited liability company structure, rather than a corporation.

PL 86-272

Public Law 86-272 (PL 86-272) is a federal law which forbids a state from charging a net income tax on a company whose only activities in that state consist of soliciting orders for sales of tangible and personal property which are filled from outside the state. The law, however, does not provide any regulation on businesses that sell services or intangible property or on states who have business taxes besides income tax.

UDITPA

The Uniform Division of Income for Tax Purposes Act (UDITPA) gives a method for the division of income for tax purposes across multiple tax jurisdictions. It applies to income generated from business activity that is not income from either a financial organization or a public utility, or individual income for personal services. Income is allocated among all the states and foreign nations having jurisdiction to enforce a net income tax, even if they do not in fact enforce any net income tax. If the allocation method outlined in the UDITPA does not fairly represent the amount of activity or transactions done by the business in certain states, then the UDITPA permits a different allocation method which must be approved by the tax administrator for each state.

Changes in Multi-State Income Allocation Since UDITPA

While the Uniform Division of Income for Tax Purposes Act (UDITPA), enacted in 1957, required that income be allocated according to (a) percentage of sales, (b) percentage of tangible property, and (c) percentage of payroll paid in different states—all three factors being equally weighted—this has changed in the last several years, varying by states. Some states utilize the original three-factor apportionment method, while other states double-weight the sales factor or give it a very high weight relative to the other two factors (e.g. 95%). Some states have exclusively used the percentage of sales as an allocation factor.

U.S. Taxation of Multinational Transactions

Multinational businesses will have various transactions executed between different entities within the business (e.g., a foreign subsidiary paying dividends to a U.S. parent), the terms of which fall under the heading of **transfer pricing**. The IRS requires that transfer pricing occur according to how unrelated parties in an arm's-length transaction would price the transactions; otherwise it will adjust these prices to arrive at a more accurate income for the entities in question.Additionally, when paying taxable income from the U.S. to nonresident aliens, special *withholding* rules apply. Ordinarily, all U.S.-source income must have 30% withheld and reported on Form 1042 and Form 1042-S. The U.S. has certain income tax treaties which permit a lower rate of withholding, but it is the alien's obligation to tell this to the business along with Form W-8BEN. The penalties for violating this can be steep.Also important is the concept of tax nexus due to **permanent establishment**. According to certain treaties, a business may gain business in a country without generating any income tax liability to that country, but only if such income is not attributable to a permanent establishment of the business within that country. However, businesses earning U.S. income without any permanent establishment in the U.S. are generally required to file a return, simply to report that no tax liability is due.

Treasury Regulations

Treasury regulations are rules issued by the U.S. Treasury under congressional authority which provide interpretations of the Internal Revenue Code (IRC). The regulations issued can be in three different forms: proposed, temporary, or final, with only the final regulations having the abiding force of law; temporary regulations have the force of law until their expiration, which is ordinarily three years after their issuance. Among the treasury regulations are procedural, interpretive, and legislative regulations. Procedural regulations explain internal IRS conduct and describe the information which must be reported by taxpayers. Interpretive regulations clarify and expand upon legislation which is based upon committee reports. Legislative regulations delegate the authority to legislate unto the Treasury Department, which then provide supplementary details for particular issues.

Revenue Rulings, Revenue Procedures, and Letter Rulings

Revenue rulings provide guidance for particular situations for taxpayers, tax preparers, and IRS personnel. They are issued by the IRS national office, and usually provide examples of how the IRS applies a certain law. Revenue procedures are similar to revenue rulings in their issuance and purpose, but they are more administrative in their content. Letter rulings are outlines or descriptions of how the IRS will treat a certain transaction for tax purposes. They are issued for a fee for particular taxpayers and particular transactions—that is, they are not issued to address certain kinds or categories of transactions, only one particular transaction—yet they bear authority in practice for other transactions (in which case the details about a particular taxpayer are removed). Letter rulings sometimes can be changed into revenue rulings depending on their helpfulness and applicability.

Determination Letters and TAM

Determination letters are similar to letter rulings. They are not published, and they are issued by regional IRS offices for taxpayers who request them. They explain how the IRS will deal with a certain transaction, usually a transaction that is already completed or a class of transactions which are recurring in nature. Technical advice memoranda (TAM) must also be requested by taxpayers, and can be requested by IRS agents. The IRS national office issues TAM for guidance of issues related to audits. They cannot be technically cited as precedents, but they still wield much authority in practice for penalties concerned with tax accuracy.

Federal Taxation of Property Transactions

Capital Assets

The Internal Revenue Code does not define the term capital asset, but it does explain what items are not considered to be capital assets. Property held for personal use and investment property are included in capital assets. Capital assets are not:

- Business-use property that is depreciated
- Real estate used in a business
- Inventory or other property that is held for customer sales through the normal course of business
- Notes receivable and other accounts obtained through the normal course of business
- Copyrights
- Compositions of art or literature that the taxpayer has developed
- Publications by the federal government obtained by methods other than purchasing at regular price
- Business supplies

Property Basis for Property Acquired as Gift or by Inheritance

For property gifts, the property basis is determined by the donor's property basis, gift tax paid, property value, and date of the gift. Property received as a gift has a holding period beginning on the date that the donor obtained the property. For property received from a decedent, the property basis is the value of the property at the date of death or at the alternate valuation date. The holding basis is ordinarily considered to be long-term.

Guidelines for Amortization Expense

Amortization is available for intangible assets. Intangible assets that may be amortized include patents, copyrights, research and development expenses, and business startup costs. Business start-up costs may be amortized only if the taxpayer is not already in that type of business; if the taxpayer does not go through with the business, these expenses are not deductible. If the taxpayer is already in that type of business, business start-up costs are expensed during the year in which they are incurred. Research and development expenses may be expensed over a five-year period. Copyrights and patents may be expensed over the asset's useful life. If the code does not state the amortization period explicitly, intangible assets are amortized over their useful lives (usually fifteen years).

Depreciation Guidelines

Taxpayers are permitted to write off specific asset costs for business assets or assets held to generate income. This write-off usually is done by depreciation, amortization, or depletion, depending on the asset type. This "write-off" provides for deterioration of property over time.

- Property placed in service between 1981 and 1986 is subject to the accelerated cost recovery system, or ACRS. Property placed in service beginning in 1987 is subject to the modified accelerated cost recovery system, or MACRS. MACRS does not use the salvage value in depreciation calculations.

- Excluding natural resources, tangible assets, such as furniture or buildings, are depreciated. Intangible assets, such as patents, are amortized. Natural resources, such as timber and oil, are depleted. If the taxpayer cannot determine the asset's useful life, there is typically no asset write-off.
- Depreciation amounts are determined by evaluating the asset type, useful life, method of depreciation, and averaging convention. The asset type is determined by the Asset Depreciation Range (ADR) guidelines.

Depletion Expense Guidelines

Depletion, which is similar to depreciation, may be taken by the owner of the natural resource for natural resources that can be used up. Depletion is deducted for AGI. Development costs and intangible drilling costs may be either capitalized and depleted or charged off as an expense in the year the expense was incurred. It usually benefits the taxpayer to elect to expense these costs as the percentage depletion is computed with no consideration for the basis; if capitalized, these costs can be lost as a deduction. Depletion can be computed by either cost depletion or percentage depletion:

- Percentage depletion: calculated by using a designated percentage in the Internal Revenue Code multiplied by the property's gross income
- Cost depletion: calculated by [(adjusted basis/number of recoverable units) * number of units sold during the year] in which the adjusted basis is calculated by subtracting accumulated depletion from the asset cost

Transactions Consisting of Nontaxable Exchange of Property

A nontaxable exchange of property results in a change in form, but not substance, of the economic position of the taxpayer. Realized gains or losses are not recognized in a nontaxable exchange; recognition occurs when the property received is disposed of in a taxable transaction, which happens by giving the replacement property a carryover basis. Important issues in a nontaxable exchange include the effect of boot on the gain recognition.

The code has guidelines for nontaxable exchange treatment if the following conditions are met:

- The property is like-kind property, which means it is the same class of property.
- The transaction is an exchange.
- The property transferred and the property received are held either as an investment or for business use.

For a transaction to meet the criteria of a like-kind exchange, the exchange must be finished within 180 days after the old property was given up (no later than the tax return due date for the tax year that the old property was given up), and the new property must be obtained within 45 days following the time that the old property was given up. The like-kind exchange provision covered in §1031 is not an elective provision.

Net Capital Losses and Worthless Securities

Short-term capital losses that are carried over to the present year remain short-term and are added to the current year short-term items. Short-term capital losses should be used prior to the use of long-term losses. Long-term net capital losses function as a long-term capital loss carryover to be included with other current year long-term items. Long-term capital losses carried over are first netted with the current year 28% capital gains, then 25% capital gains, etc. The capital loss deduction is restricted to the lesser of capital losses greater than capital gains or $3,000; the maximum deduction for married filing separately taxpayers is $1,500. In calculating the net capital loss carryover, the net capital loss is decreased by the lesser of adjusted taxable income or $3,000 ($1,500 for married filing separately taxpayers). If a worthless security is a capital asset, the security loss resulting from an exchange or sale is considered to happen on the last day of the taxable year. If securities and stocks are from an 80% or more owned corporate subsidiary that receives over 90% of its gross receipts from sources that are active-type, the resulting loss is considered to be an ordinary loss.

Real Property vs. Personal Property and Personal Property Acquisitions

Real property includes land, as well as plant life and vegetation. Personal property can be either tangible or intangible. Tangible personal property can be moved and physically owned. Intangible personal property does not have physical substance and includes stocks, bonds, goodwill, computer programs, trademarks, copyrights, and patents. Personal property can be acquired through wills and inheritance. This would be done according to a will if the will is valid at the time of death. Otherwise, if there is no will, the property is handled according to the state. Personal property can also be acquired through gifts, which are ownership rights that are voluntarily transferred without consideration. This can be done in a last will and testament or during a donor's lifetime. An *inter vivos* gift is a current, irrevocable transfer during the lifetime of the donor. For a gift to be complete, there must be delivery from the donor, donative intent, and the donee's acceptance. Donative intent is the donor's intent of giving the gift. Gifts *causa mortis* occur when death seems to be close, due to an illness or trauma. If death does not occur from the illness or trauma, the gift is automatically revoked.

Bailments

A bailment exists whenever one person delivers personal property in trust to another person under a contract, express or implied, for a specific purpose. The bailment is established by the bailed property being brought into the bailee's possession. The bailee is responsible for following the owner's directions in either returning the bailed property or getting rid of the bailed property. A bailee has the right to use the property in bailment only for purposes of the bailment. Should the property be used with the owner's authorization, the bailee is liable. A bailment requires that the bailee carry out his duty of care with the bailed property. Bailments may be for the bailor's benefit, for the bailee's benefit, and for their mutual benefit. Bailments may be discontinued if the bailment objective is carried out, if the bailed property is not used as intended by the bailee, or if the bailee and bailor agree to terminate the bailment.

Netting Capital Gains and Losses

Capital gains and losses are netted to determine the existence of either a net capital loss or a net capital gain. To begin the netting process, short-term capital gains (STCG) and short-term capital losses (STCL) are netted; long-term capital gains (LTCG) and long-term capital losses (LTCL) are netted together. The results are a net short-term capital gain or loss and a net long-term capital gain or loss; these two are netted together to determine the net capital gain or net capital loss. Net capital gains are included in gross income.

Capital Gains Tax Guidelines for Individual Taxpayers

The short-term capital gains tax rate is the same as any individual's ordinary income tax rate, but the long-term capital gains tax rate is not. Instead, the long-term capital gains tax rate is either 0%, 15%, or 20%. Prior to the TCJA these brackets aligned with the income thresholds for the ordinary income tax brackets, but post-TCJA they have their own brackets.

§ 1231 Netting Calculation in Property Transactions

All gains and losses resulting from casualty and theft for long-term property should be netted. If the losses are greater than the gains, they should be treated as ordinary losses and gains; these ordinary losses and gains should not be used to offset § 1231 gains and losses. If gains are greater than losses, the net gain will be netted with other § 1231 gains and losses. Excluding theft and casualty net losses, the remaining § 1231 gains and losses should be netted together. If total losses are greater than total gains, all gains and losses should be treated as ordinary gains and losses. If gains are greater than the losses, the § 1231 net gain should be treated as a long-term capital gain. The net § 1231 gain will be handled as ordinary income up to the amount of net § 1231 losses that have not been recaptured for the past five taxable years.

§ 1231 Assets in Property Transactions

The provisions of § 1231 are applicable to the sale or exchange of property used in a trade or business, as well as specific involuntary conversions. These properties used in a trade or business are not classified as capital assets, since the assets are either depreciable property or real property and are referred to as § 1231 assets. To qualify as § 1231 assets, these assets must have been held for over a year. The code has guidelines for depreciation recapture in Sections 291, 1245, and 1250 before Section 1231 becomes effective. Gain is taxed in the same manner as ordinary income to the amount of previous depreciation deductions. Section 1231 provides that if gains are greater than losses for business assets, capital gain and loss rules apply. Property disposal net gains may sometimes be handled as long-term capital gains for § 1231 assets. If real property or depreciable property used in a trade or business is disposed of creating a net loss, § 1231 provides that the loss should be handled as an ordinary loss, which can be deducted for AGI. The code provides that § 1231 long-term gains and long-term losses must be netted together; net long-term gains are considered long-term capital gains, which are used to offset any capital losses. Short-term gains or losses from property held for trade or business use are treated as ordinary gains and losses.

Business Property Gains and Losses

Gains and losses can be categorized into the following groups:

- Ordinary gains and losses
- § 1231 gains and losses resulting from theft or casualty
- § 1231 gains and losses (excluding those resulting from theft or casualty)
- Capital asset gains and losses (excluding those resulting from theft or casualty)

§ 1231 gains are considered ordinary income as much as is determined by the depreciation recapture from Sections 291, 1245, and 1250. After calculating recapture of depreciation, net § 1231 gains and losses resulting from theft or casualty of property used in a trade or business. In cases of the losses being greater than the gains, ordinary treatment should be applied. In instances of gains being greater than losses, the net gain should be netted with other § 1231 gains and losses. Following depreciation recapture, any leftover § 1231 gains and losses (excluding those resulting from theft or casualty) will be added to any net gains resulting from theft or casualty. If losses are greater than gains, the gains and losses are treated as ordinary. If gains are greater than losses, the net gain will be treated as a long-term capital gain.

Capital Gains and Losses Resulting from Property Transactions and Classification of Gains and Losses

Capital gains and capital losses are required to be distinguished from other kinds of gains and losses for tax purposes. Net capital losses may be deducted for married filing jointly taxpayers up to $3,000. Single taxpayers may deduct up to $3,000 in net capital losses as well. Ordinary gains may be taxed at a higher rate than long-term capital gains. Gain and loss recognition is classified according to the property tax status, the method of property disposition, and the property holding period. These factors determine how the net capital gains will be taxed. Property tax status will be one of the following: ordinary asset, capital asset, or a § 1231 asset. Property may be disposed of via exchange, sale, theft, casualty, or condemnation; the most common method of property disposition is via sale. Typically, property disposition triggers capital gains and losses. Property holding periods are either short-term, which is one year or less, or long-term, which is greater than one year. The holding period does not include the acquisition date but does include the disposition date of the property.

Corporation Capital Gains and Losses

Classification between long-term and short-term gains and losses is determined from the holding period of the asset that has been either exchanged or sold. Corporations will net long-term capital gains and losses every year, which will result in either a net long-term capital gain or a net long-term capital loss. Short-term capital gains and losses are also netted together to produce either a net short-term capital gain or a net short-term capital loss.

From the netting process, here are the possible results:

- A short-term capital gain and a net long-term capital gain; these are not netted together.
- A net short-term capital loss and a net long-term capital loss; these are not netted together.
- A net short-term capital gain and a net long-term capital loss; these are netted to result in either a net capital loss or a net capital gain.
- A net short-term capital loss and a net long-term capital gain; these are netted to produce either a net capital loss or a net capital gain.
- Corporations treat net capital gains as taxable income; there is no favorable treatment for capital gains.

Involuntary Conversions

If a taxpayer experiences an involuntary conversion of property, the taxpayer may postpone any gain recognition that was realized in the conversion. Involuntary conversion occurs from theft, damage, or condemnation of property of the taxpayer. The involuntary conversion provision covered in § 1033 of the Code is an elective provision. If the replacement property cost is equal to or greater than the gain realized, the gain realized is not recognized. If the replacement property cost is less than the gain realized, the realized gain is recognized to the deficiency amount. Loss recognition is no different for involuntary conversions. The taxpayer may choose to not recognize gain if the taxpayer receives payment and realizes gain, and if similar or related in service or use property replaces the converted property. Property that is immediately converted into similar or related in service or use property requires that the taxpayer not recognize any gain. Replacement property guidelines are more limited than like-kind property guidelines. Taxpayers usually have two years following the taxable year-end to realize gain resulting from the involuntary conversion by replacing the converted property. Property received in an involuntary conversion will have the holding period of the old property, if the old property was either a § 1231 asset or capital asset.

Basis of Like-Kind Property Received

The calculation of the basis of like-kind property received:

+ Recognized gain

+ Boot basis Recognized loss Value of boot received

= Like-kind property received basis

Boot is money or property that is not like-kind. If boot is received, the boot basis will be the value of the boot on the exchange date. If boot is received, realized gain will be recognized. Recognized gain will be the lesser of the realized gain or the boot received. If there is a realized loss, receipt of boot does not cause any recognition. Giving of boot does not usually cause any recognition; if cash is the boot, any gain or loss that is realized is not recognized. Any assumption of liabilities in the exchange is treated as a boot exchange. If boot is received, the boot has a new holding period beginning on the exchange date. The holding period of property given up in a property exchange will carry over and be added to the holding period of the like-kind property received.

Recapture Provisions for Property Transactions

Recapture Provisions in Section 1250 for Property Transactions

Section 1250 property is usually depreciable real property that is not subject to Section 1245. This includes intangible real property, such as leaseholds of § 1250 property. Section 1250 is not applicable for real property that has been sold at a loss, which is usually classified as a § 1231 loss. Section 1250 recapture is often described as partial recapture.

Short-term § 1250 property gains resulting from disposition are recaptured as ordinary income equal to the amount of all depreciation. Long-term § 1250 property gains are recaptured as ordinary income equal to the amount of post-1969 additional depreciation. Additional depreciation is the excess of accelerated depreciation that has been deducted over depreciation that would have been deducted had the straight-line depreciation method been used.

Recapture Provisions in Section 291 for Property Transactions

For corporations, ordinary income resulting from a § 1250 property disposition is increased by 20% of the additional amount that would have been treated as ordinary income if the § 1250 property had been § 1245 property.

Related Party Transactions

Related party transactions are any exchanges which occur with family members, exchanges between an individual and any pass-through entity or corporation of which he has over 50% ownership, whether direct or indirect, exchanges between two corporations which are members of the same controlled group, and exchanges between trusts and grantors, fiduciary trustees, beneficiaries, or corporations of which the trust grantor has over 50% ownership. The Internal Revenue Code (IRC) restricts related party transaction gains and losses. Losses resulting from related party transactions are not deductible; in cases of property sold to a related party, then sold again to a nonrelated party, the resulting gain from the second transaction must be decreased by the previously disallowed loss to calculate the final gain on sale.

Federal Estate Tax Guidelines

The gross estate is comprised of the total property at fair market value at the time of death (or at an alternate valuation date). This includes the following:

- Jointly held property
- Transfers that were planned at death at the fair market value
- Life insurance proceeds from policies in which the decedent had the right to change the beneficiary or policies that are payable to the decedent's estate
- Transfers with revocable transfers and retained life estates
- Property in which the decedent possessed a general power of appointment

- Decedent's income
- Estate tax returns must be filed for estates which have combined gross assets and prior taxable gifts of over $12.92 million, as of 2023.
- Property basis for property received from a decedent is usually the property fair market value at the decedent's death date or the alternate valuation date.

Federal Gift Tax Guidelines

For gifts, the donee must be able to acquire and own the gift, the donee must accept the gift, the donor must have intended to give the gift and be competent, and the gift must be delivered to the donee. All property transfers given by citizens or residents of the USA in a gratuitous manner are subject to the federal gift tax. The property location is irrelevant. To qualify as a property transfer given in a gratuitous manner, the gift must not involve consideration. The donor's basis for gain is the property basis in addition to gift taxes due to property appreciation. For losses, the amount is the lesser of the gift's fair market value as of the date of the gift or the gain basis.

Annual Exclusions Regarding Gift Tax Deductions

Donors are permitted an annual exclusion of $17,000 per donee for present interest gifts in 2023. If a married couple gives a gift, the recipients may be treated as two separate donors and double the annual exclusion. The unified tax credit is still allowed. Gift tax returns are filed on a calendar year basis and are due the following April 15.

Calculation of Federal Estate Taxes

The calculation of federal estate taxes is a function of the gross value of the estate, the debt owed by the decedent at the point of death, the expenses which will be incurred when settling the estate, and any other applicable deductions. After determining the gross value of the estate, one should subtract all debts (including mortgages, credit card debts, etc.) and expenses (funeral expenses, attorney expenses, etc.), charitable transfers, and transfers to one's spouse to determine the net estate. From the net estate, one subtracts the federal estate tax exemption, which is $12.92 million for 2023. Due to the large exemption, most people do not need to pay a federal estate tax.

Marital Deductions

When calculating estate tax, the marital deduction is generally unlimited; the decedent could conceivably give the entire estate (i.e., the net estate, not gross), without reducing any of it, to the spouse. The one limitation to the marital deduction is that the deduction interest should be a non-terminable interest in property that is included within the gross estate. Terminable interests are interests that will expire after a given amount of time or some future event's occurrence (such as the spouse's remarriage).

Unified Tax Credits

Unified tax credits apply to gifts given away during one's lifetime: if one gives away money in excess of the annual gift tax exclusion amount, one can choose whether to pay a gift tax on that excess amount or avert the gift tax by treating it as unified credit. However, if unified credit is used, then the exemption amount to reduce one's estate tax upon one's death is less than before. The term "unified credit" arises from the credit that serves to interconnect the federal estate tax and federal gift tax systems.

Important Terms

Property Gains and Losses Terminology

Amount realized — Money received in addition to the value of other property received

Adjusted basis — Original basis of property that is adjusted to the disposition date; calculated by:

Cost or adjusted basis at acquisition date

+ Capital additions Capital recoveries

= Disposition date adjusted basis

Capital additions — Improvements to property

Capital recoveries — Depreciation, cost recovery allowances, bond premiums that can be amortized, specific corporate distributions, thefts, and casualties

Realized gain — Realized amount is greater than the adjusted basis of property

Realized loss — Realized amount is less than the adjusted basis of the property

Recognized gain — Realized gain included in the gross income of a taxpayer

Recognized loss — Deductible realized loss

Depreciation Terminology

Averaging convention — used to determine the amount of depreciation for the year that the property was placed in service or disposed of

Half-month convention — real property placed in service is considered to have been placed in service at the midpoint of the month.

Half-year convention — under MACRS, personal property is considered to have been placed in service or disposed of at the taxable year midpoint; this methodology does not permit any depreciation recording for assets disposed of in the same year they were placed in service

Midquarter convention — if greater than 40% of the property value (excluding eligible real estate) was placed in service during the last quarter of the year, the property is considered to have been placed in service or disposed in the middle of the quarter in which it was placed in service or disposed of

Recovery property — all property, excluding land, intangible assets, and property that the taxpayer chooses to depreciate using a depreciation method that is not described by a time period.

Federal Taxation of Individuals

Items Included in Gross Income

Unless otherwise excluded, gross income includes all income from all sources. Returns of capital and income assignments are not recognized in gross income. Income must be realized and considered to be a taxable event to be included in gross income. Gross income specifically includes:

- Alimony – Child support is not included as gross income; prior to the 2017 Tax Cuts & Jobs Act (TCJA), alimony payments were income to the recipient and deductible to the payer, but with the TCJA, for divorces enacted in 2019 or later alimony payments are nondeductible for the payer and excluded from the recipient's net income.
- Awards and prizes, excluding employee achievement awards
- Unemployment
- Social security - If a taxpayer's income is greater than a specific amount, up to 85% of the taxpayer's social security income should be included in gross income.
- Compensation for services provided (commissions and salary)
- Includes employer-paid life insurance premiums except for up to $50,000 of group term-life insurance coverage
- Expenses reimbursed by employer or paid by the employee, unless the employee is required to report the expenses to the employer; in this case, the expenses qualify as deductible business expenses
- Supplemental unemployment benefits from an employer
- Business income
- Dividends
- Interest from banks, tax refunds, and imputed interest on below-market loans
- Income from S corporations or partnerships
- Royalties and rental income
- Gain from sale of real estate or securities
- Unless excluded, income from a discharge of indebtedness
- Stock options - Incentive stock options are treated in the taxpayer's favor; stock option granting or exercising does not cause a taxable event. Certain criteria must be met for the stock option to receive favorable treatment. If a nonqualified stock option's fair market value can be determined, it is included in gross income.
- Gambling proceeds
- Tax benefits – If a tax deduction from a previous year is recovered in the current year, it should be included in gross income to the extent that a tax benefit was derived from the prior deduction of the recovered item.
- Illegal income

Items Excluded from Gross Income

Items excluded from gross income are:

- Supplements to wages and salary
- Military benefits
- Fringe benefits
- Foreign earned income
- Donative items

- Benefits available for the elderly
- Welfare and personal items
- Items available to investors
- Miscellaneous benefits

Welfare and personal items include items such as foster care reimbursements; property settlement resulting from divorce proceedings; payments for injury, public assistance, or sickness; child support payments; and the portion of pensions or annuities reflecting a return of capital. Donative items include items such as scholarships, gifts, inheritances, and life insurance proceeds (up to policy face amount) paid in cases of death. Supplements to wages and salary include the following:

- Military benefits, such as combat pay or housing benefits
- Fringe benefits, such as employee discounts, employer-paid health and accident benefits, child adoption expenses, dependent care, employee achievement awards, qualified moving expense reimbursement, cafeteria plans, medical savings accounts, parsonage rental value, long-term care insurance; employer's qualified education assistance, etc.
- Foreign earned income - Qualifying U.S. citizens and resident aliens who live and work abroad can elect to exclude all or part of foreign salary or wages, or amounts received as compensation for personal services. In addition, certain foreign housing costs may also qualify for exclusion or a deduction.

Benefits available to the elderly include social security benefits, unless the taxpayer achieves a certain level of income. Items available to investors include state and local government obligation interest and specific business stock. Miscellaneous benefits include gain from sale of personal residence, income from indebtedness discharge if certain criteria are met, bonds for educational savings, and qualified state tuition programs.

Income from a discharge of indebtedness may be excluded under certain guidelines:

- The discharge of indebtedness is a gift
- Debt is discharged as a result of bankruptcy proceedings
- Debtor is insolvent prior to and following discharge
- A shareholder discharges a corporation's debt; these cases are viewed as a capital contribution
- Student loan discharges in cases where the debtor is employed in a specific profession for a designated time period
- The discharge of indebtedness is a purchase money debt reduction; these cases are viewed as a purchase price reduction

Business Expenses

Capital Expenditures

The Internal Revenue Code (IRC) does not permit deductions for capital expenditures, which are expenses increasing value or extending life of property; these expenses are considered a cost of the property. This does not include regular repairs and maintenance, which is considered a deductible business expense. For example, roof repairs are considered repairs and maintenance, a deductible business expense. Purchasing a new roof is considered to be a capital expenditure that will be depreciated over its useful life. Expenditures pertaining to intangible assets are amortized for fifteen years.

Related Party Transactions

The IRC restricts related party transaction gains and losses. Losses resulting from related party transactions are not deductible; in cases of property sold to a related party, then sold again to a nonrelated party, the resulting gain from the second transaction must be decreased by the previously disallowed loss to calculate the final gain on sale.

Illegal Business Expenses

Normal operating expenses are deductible; fines, illegal payments, and bribes to public officials are not deductible.

Business Use of Home

Deductible if a home is used as the exclusive, regular, and principal place of business.

Qualified Business Income Deduction

The Tax Cuts & Jobs Act, to provide tax benefits to sole proprietorships and owners of pass-through tax entities (e.g., partnerships and S corporations), created a deduction for 20% of one's qualified business income (QBI). QBI excludes income from "specified service" trades or businesses, defined as including fields like law, accounting, athletics, health, and financial services. Additionally, the deduction is limited by the greater of (a) 50% of the taxpayer's allocated share of W-2 wages or (b) 25% of such wages plus 2.5% of the undepreciated basis of the taxpayer's business property. Both these limitations—the exclusion of "specified service" income and the wages and asset limitations—apply only for taxpayers whose income (as of 2023) exceeds a $364,200 threshold ($182,100 for single or head-of-household taxpayers), phasing out entirely when their income reaches $464,200 ($232,100 for single or head-of-household taxpayers). This deduction is taken "below the line," that is, after AGI. On the 1040 it is after the standard/itemized deduction line but before taxable income.

Credits and Deductions

Tax credits reduce a taxpayer's tax liability dollar-for-dollar. Frequently used tax credits include the child tax credit and earned income credit. Deductions are divided into two categories: deductions <u>for</u> Adjusted Gross Income (AGI) and deductions <u>from</u> AGI. Tax deductions reduce taxable income, which is used to calculate tax liability. All deductions from or for AGI are reflected on pages 1 and 2 of Form 1040. All deductions for AGI are shown on page 1; adjusted gross income is the last line on page 1. The first amount on page 2 is also AGI. The next amounts are one's standard or itemized deductions and the qualified business income deduction; the final calculation is taxable income.

Reporting of Taxes for Pass-Through Entities

While corporations have double taxation as a drawback, pass-through entities avoid being taxed at the corporate level and pass through the taxable income straight to the owners. For instance, if some partnership's earnings before taxes (EBT) is $500,000, and if each of the two partners owns 50%, then they both will owe taxes on $250,000. (Thus, if there is a 30% tax rate, they would each owe $75,000.) This tax obligation is determined by the ownership interest, so each of the partners would have an individual taxable income of $250,000 even if that is not how the income was in fact distributed. Besides partnerships, other examples of pass-through entities are sole proprietorships, S corporations, master limited partnerships (MLPs), limited liability partnerships (LLPs), and limited liability companies (LLCs).

Standard Deduction

For 2023, the standard deduction is $27,700 for married filing jointly taxpayers; $20,800 for head of household taxpayers; $13,850 for single taxpayers; and $13,850 for married filing separately taxpayers. The standard deduction for a dependent for 2023 will be the dependent's earned income plus $400, though it must be at least $1,150 and at most $12,950.

To compute a taxpayer's taxable income, the standard deduction (or itemized deductions) plus exemption amounts are subtracted from Adjusted Gross Income (AGI). Individuals are required to file a tax return if gross income is equal to the standard deduction plus allowable personal exemptions. Excluding surviving spouses, single taxpayers ages 65 and over or blind have a $1,850 standard deduction in addition (as of 2023). If the taxpayer is blind and 65 or over, the taxpayer will receive an additional standard deduction of the same amount, totaling $3,700. Married taxpayers age 65 and over or blind receive an additional $1,500 per person in addition to the standard deduction during 2023. If a dependent is also blind or 65 and over, the taxpayer may claim the dependent standard deduction plus the additional standard deduction allowed for the blind or elderly.

Deductions for AGI

Deductions for Adjusted Gross Income (AGI) may be claimed by the taxpayer regardless of whether the taxpayer itemizes deductions. Most deductions for AGI shown on page 1 of Form 1040 are supported by attached schedules. Deductions for AGI include the following:

- Designated contributions for pension, profit-sharing, or self-employed individual's annuity plans;
- Trade or business expenses;
- Moving expenses;
- Interest paid on student loans, up to $2,500;
- Property sale and exchange losses;
- 50% of taxes for self-employment;
- Discrimination lawsuit costs;
- Expenses associated with royalties and rent;
- Penalties resulting from early withdrawal from time deposits;
- Jury duty pay given to the employer

After taking deductions for AGI from gross income, the result is the taxpayer's AGI. AGI helps to determine the deductible amounts that will be allowed for miscellaneous itemized deductions, medical deductions, charitable contributions, and casualty losses, since many itemized deductions (such as medical expenses) are limited to amounts greater than certain percentages of AGI. When AGI increases, these itemized deductions decrease.

Deductions from AGI

Deductions from Adjusted Gross Income (AGI) benefit the taxpayer only if he itemizes, meaning that allowable deductions are greater than the standard deduction available to the taxpayer. If total deductions from AGI do not exceed the standard deduction, the taxpayer will not receive a tax benefit from these deductions. Itemized deductions are reflected on page 2 of Form 1040 and Schedule A. Deductions from AGI include:

- Medical expenses (exceeding 7.5% of AGI)
- Mortgage interest on a personal residence (only on loans up to $750,000, per the TCJA)
- Charitable contributions (no greater than a specific % of AGI)

- Real estate taxes, as well as state and local taxes

Deductions for Interest and Legal Expenses

Interest deduction classification: Interest is considered deductible for AGI if the associated indebtedness is for a business, as well as royalty or rent income. Indebtedness of a personal nature, such as home mortgage interest, is deducted from AGI as an itemized deduction and is reported on Form 1040 Schedule A, if the taxpayer itemizes. Generally, the source of the funds is used to determine the interest expense classification.

Legal expenses: These may be deducted only if a taxpayer proves that the expenses are directly pertaining to a business or income-producing transaction. Legal expenses incurred for personal use are not deductible.

Expenses Associated with Rental and Royalty Property

Rental and royalty property expenses are deductible for AGI. If a taxpayer rents a vacation home and uses it for personal use, the deductible expenses are calculated by:

[(# of days rented/total days used) * total expenses]

If a vacation home is used as a residence, the deductible expenses are restricted to rental income minus deductions that are generally allowed for taxes, interest, and casualty losses. If the vacation home is used as a residence and the taxpayer rents out the vacation home for less than 15 days during the year, the income is not reported and the expenses are non-deductible.

Charitable Contributions

A charitable contribution is a gift made by the taxpayer to a qualified organization. Charitable contributions must have the donee's acceptance, a lack of consideration, and a donative intent. The Internal Revenue Code (IRC) doesn't provide for deductibility of services contributed to a qualified organization. Other nondeductible items include the cost of tuition, blood donations to a blood bank, gifts to individuals, and dues paid to social organizations, such as lodges or country clubs. Taxpayers using either accrual or cash accounting methods must deduct charitable contributions in the year in which they are paid. Excess charitable contributions may be carried over for five years. Taxpayers must receive written proof from the qualified charitable organization to deduct contributions of $250 or more. For contributions of property with value between $500 and $5,000, the taxpayer is required to file Form 8283, Section A. Taxpayers making a noncash contribution worth over $5,000 are required to file Form 8283, Section B, and have a qualified appraisal done on the property. The IRC has restrictions on charitable contributions: 1. Charitable contributions are limited to 50% of Adjusted Gross Income (AGI). 2. Charitable contributions are fully deductible if equal to or less than 20% of AGI. 3. For charitable contributions exceeding 20% of AGI, depending on the property type and the organization type, the deduction will be 20%, 30%, or 50% of AGI.

Tax Characteristics of Roth IRA

Contributions to a Roth IRA are not deductible; Roth IRA qualified distributions are not taxable. For 2023, the maximum Roth IRA contribution is $6,500; for taxpayers ages 50 and over, the maximum Roth IRA contribution is $7,500. There are phase-out rules for Roth IRAs. For 2023, Roth IRA eligibility is phased out for joint filers when the AGI range is $218,000–$228,000; for single filers, the AGI phase-out range is $138,000–$153,000. Taxpayers are allowed to receive tax-free Roth IRA withdrawals following a five-year holding period as long as one the following requirements are met:

- The Roth IRA distribution is used for a qualified first-time home purchase.
- The Roth IRA participant becomes disabled.
- The Roth IRA distribution is made on or following the participant's age of 59½.
- The beneficiary receives the distribution following the participant's death.

ITEMIZED DEDUCTIONS

TAXES AND CASUALTY LOSSES

State and local taxes, as well as foreign taxes, are deductible. Fees are usually not deductible, unless they are incurred through the normal course of business. *Ad valorem* property taxes are deductible, which means that the tax assessment is derived from the property value. Annual real estate taxes are divided between a seller and buyer; each pays his *pro rata* share based on the number of days he held the property. Real property taxes are deductible. Taxpayers have the choice of deducting either state and local income taxes, or state and local general sales taxes, up to a maximum of $10,000 in either case (per the TCJA). The following taxes are not deductible: federal income taxes, federal employment taxes paid by an employee; and estate or gift taxes. Businesses may deduct the following expenses: employment taxes, gasoline taxes, and federal excise taxes on air transportation, tires, telephone service, and automobiles.

Each deductible personal casualty loss must be reduced by $100. Losses are calculated as the lesser of the property's adjusted basis or the decrease in property value caused by the casualty. Gains and losses are considered capital gains and losses if theft gains and personal casualty gains are greater than losses, following the $100 floor applied to every loss. Per the TCJA, only casualty losses from federally declared disasters are deductible, although casualty losses from other events can be used to offset casualty gains from such events. If deductible losses, following the $100 floor applied to every loss, are greater than the gains, then the losses are netted with the gains, the total of personal casualty losses is decreased by 10% of AGI, and that amount is deductible to AGI.

MISCELLANEOUS ITEMIZED DEDUCTIONS

Prior to the TCJA, miscellaneous itemized deductions were deductible for the total greater than 2% of AGI. These expenses included safe deposit box fees, investment expenses as discussed in Internal Revenue Code (IRC) §212, unreimbursed employee expenses, and fees for tax return preparation. Following the passage of the TCJA, none of these expenses are deductible.

The following expenses are not deductible:

- Personal expenses
- Illegal transactions
- Expenses to bury others (funeral expenses)
- Homeowner's insurance
- Licenses for automobiles
- Donations made to political organizations
- Marriage licenses
- Legal expenses for personal reasons
- Tax penalties and fines
- Work commute
- Life insurance
- Rent on residence

Interest Expenses

Deductible interest includes investment interest, home mortgage interest, and qualified education loan interest. Qualified education loan interest can be deducted for AGI up to $2,500. Investment interest expense deductions are restricted to the net investment income in a year. Mortgage prepayment penalties are treated as deductible interest. Home mortgage interest, or qualified residence interest, is deductible for interest which is accrued or paid on indebtedness that is secured by property that is considered the taxpayer's qualified residence during the taxable year. A taxpayer's qualified residence consists of the principal residence of the taxpayer and one other residence of the taxpayer. The principal residence must meet the criteria of the IRC §121 for nonrecognition of gain on sale. The one other residence must be either rented or used as a residence. Home mortgage interest includes home equity loan interest and acquisition indebtedness interest. With the TCJA, acquisition indebtedness interest is deductible only on loans up to $750,000, and this $750,000 amount includes home equity loans whose proceeds are used to purchase or improve the taxpayer's first or second home. (Pre-TCJA, home equity loan interest was deductible on loans up to $100,000, even if the proceeds were used for non-home-related expenses.) Mortgage company points on a home mortgage loan for the purchase or improvement of a principal residence are deductible as interest in the year paid if the points pay the lender for a loan; otherwise, the points are capitalized and amortized over the loan life.

Moving Expenses

Prior to the TCJA, moving expenses for the purpose of moving to a new place of work were deductible. The TCJA repealed this deduction outright.

Medical Expenses

Itemized deductions are deductible from Adjusted Gross Income (AGI) to calculate taxable income, if the taxpayer chooses to itemize deductions. Taxpayers can itemize medical expenses when they are incurred for the taxpayer, taxpayer's spouse, and dependents, for expenses that have not been reimbursed. Deduction is restricted to the medical expenses exceeding 7.5% of AGI. (This was previously slated to increase to 10% of AGI, but the 2021 Consolidated Appropriations Act made the 7.5% floor permanent.) Deductible medical expenses include dental care, mental care, hospital care, prescribed drugs, medical care transportation, medical insurance premiums, alcohol rehabilitation, drug rehabilitation, and special equipment, such as eyeglasses, contact lenses, hearing aids, crutches, wheelchairs, and artificial limbs. Cosmetic surgery is deductible only if it is medically required. Medical expenses may be capitalized; examples would be swimming pools or air conditioners, though they must be purchased for medical purposes. Transportation and lodging expenses are deductible (the AGI floor is applicable) when incurred to obtain medical care. Medical expenses are only deductible during the year in which they are paid. The taxpayer's accounting method is irrelevant. Medical savings account contributions are deductible for particular employees and self-employed taxpayers.

Casualty Losses

Individual taxpayers' losses are generally restricted to business losses and losses from transactions engaged in for a profit, with business losses are limited to the amount a taxpayer has "at risk." Individual taxpayers are permitted to deduct casualty losses as an itemized deduction from AGI in the year that the loss occurs. Insurance premiums for casualties are not deductible, as they are considered a personal expense. These deductible losses include those caused by theft, fire, or storm; damages to trees and other growing things on real estate, if the real estate now has a decreased value; personal residence losses due to a disaster, if the government mandates that it be either destroyed or moved. To be deductible, casualty losses must be occurrences that were unexpected, unusual, or sudden, and (per the TCJA) must be due to a federally declared disaster. Deductible casualty losses must be property damage that can be identified. Deductible casualty losses do not include damage from termites or diseases, damage to possessions resulting from lack of care of the taxpayer, losses caused by destruction in close proximity, etc. Individual taxpayers are not allowed to deduct casualty losses for a decrease in value to insured property that is not used in a business, unless the taxpayer files an insurance claim in a timely manner. Casualty losses are decreased by the amount of insurance reimbursement.

Adoption Expenses Credit and Earned Income Credit

The adoption expenses credit is a nonrefundable credit, up to $15,950 for tax year 2023, that may be carried forward for five years. This credit is intended to help taxpayers with qualifying adoption costs. The earned income credit (EIC) is intended to provide the working poor with tax equity and to offset regressive taxes. This refundable credit is also intended to help motivate low-income people to become a part of the workforce. To obtain the earned income credit, taxpayers must meet the Adjusted Gross Income (AGI) and earned income thresholds and must not use the married filing separately filing status. Some individuals without qualifying children can claim the EIC. If a taxpayer has one or more qualifying children, the taxpayer must maintain a household for more than 50% of the year for a qualifying child. Eligible earned income consists of salaries and wages, other employee compensation, and self-employment income. For tax year 2023, the maximum earned income credit permitted is $3,995 for taxpayers having one qualifying child, $6,604 for taxpayers with two qualifying children, and $7,430 for taxpayers with three or more qualifying children.

Passive Activity

Passive activity is activity from business (or income-producing) activity in which the taxpayer has not materially participated throughout the year. Rental activities are considered passive activities, regardless of how much the taxpayer participated. A limited partnership interest qualifies as passive activity.

Material Participation

The taxpayer actively participates consistently and significantly. The participation level is determined by tests provided in the passive activity regulations.

Passive Activity Credits

These may be used for offsetting tax liability resulting from passive activity income. Current credits exceeding current tax liability may be carried over into future years. If a taxpayer gets rid of a passive activity interest, unlike losses, excess credits may not be used in full and must be carried over into following years.

Rental Activity

Rental activity is an activity in which the taxpayer receives payments for the use of tangible property. Rental activity is determined by the failure of an activity in meeting one of the six exceptions presented in the passive activity regulations. Individuals actively participating in rental activity are allowed to offset up to $25,000 of non-passive income with rental real estate losses or credits. Passive loss limitations are not applicable for credits and losses for closely held C corporations and individuals who qualify for specified guidelines and materially participate in rental real estate activities.

Passive Activity Losses, Portfolio Income, and Active Income

Rules for passive losses are applicable to personal service corporations, closely held C corporations, individuals, estates, and trusts. For partnerships and S corporations, passive activity flows to the owners, and the passive loss rules apply to them. Guidelines for passive losses mandate that taxpayers separate income and losses into three groups: active, passive, and portfolio. As a general rule, passive losses may be used to offset only passive income. Even when the taxpayer is at risk to the extent of the loss, passive losses may not be deducted against activity or portfolio income. Passive losses that are not allowed as deductions may be suspended and used in later years. At-risk limitations were created to disallow taxpayers from taking loss deductions that exceed actual economic investment in an activity. In regard to borrowings, taxpayers are not considered to be at risk if either the lender (excluding the position of creditor) has an interest in the activity or the taxpayer may not be held liable personally for the debt repayment. There is an exception to this rule that concerns real property being held: a taxpayer is at risk for his portion of qualified nonrecourse financing for which real property is secured for this activity. Portfolio income includes items such as property disposition gains or losses creating portfolio income, and income out of the normal course of business resulting in interest, dividends, and royalties. Active income includes items such as wages, salaries, commissions, and other compensation for work performed, gain on sale of assets used in an active business, and business income from a business in which the taxpayer materially participates.

SIMPLE Retirement Plans

SIMPLE retirement plans are available for employers, without another qualified retirement plan, with less than 100 employees. SIMPLE plans may be designed as either a 401(k) plan or an IRA. However, the nondiscrimination and top-heavy rules that pertain to 401(k) plans are not applicable to SIMPLE plans. SIMPLE-eligible employees include employees who were compensated at least $5,000 in two prior years and expect to be compensated a minimum of $5,000 during the current year. For 2023, SIMPLE plan contributions may be made by employees up to $15,500 of their salaries (before taxes). Employees over age 50 may make additional catch-up contributions of $3,500. Employee contributions are stated as a compensation percentage instead of a fixed dollar amount. SIMPLE plan employers must match a portion of the employee's contributions. All SIMPLE plan contributions are fully vested; however, if withdrawals are taken during the first two years of the employee's plan entry, there is a 25% early withdrawal tax.

Tax Implications of Traditional IRA

Taxpayers not participating in a qualified retirement plan are allowed to begin a tax-deductible IRA. For 2023, taxpayers are allowed to deduct IRA contributions up to $6,500; married filing jointly taxpayers are permitted to contribute up to $6,500 for each of their IRAs (they must have separate IRAs). Taxpayers are allowed to make nondeductible contributions. There is no penalty for withdrawals to pay for qualified higher education or first-time home purchases. Traditional IRAs do not have a phase-out if neither the taxpayer nor his spouse participates in either a Keogh plan or an employer-sponsored plan. If the taxpayer participates in another qualified plan, the traditional IRA deduction restriction phases out proportionately between specific AGI ranges. In 2023, for married filing jointly taxpayers, the AGI range is $116,000–$136,000; for single taxpayers, the AGI range is $73,000–$83,000. If the taxpayer does not participate in another qualified plan, but the taxpayer's spouse participates in another qualified plan, the AGI range for the joint AGI is $218,000–$228,000. For 2023, taxpayers age 50 and above are permitted to make extra "catch-up" contributions of $1,000 to a traditional IRA. Therefore, taxpayers ages 50 and over may make a total IRA deductible contribution of $7,500.

Filing Statuses of Individual Taxpayers

Filing statuses available to individual taxpayers are as follows:

- Single
- Married filing jointly – May be married at the time of death of a spouse or at year-end.

- Married filing separately - May be married at the time of death of a spouse or at year-end.
- Head of household – For unmarried individuals maintaining a household for a dependent; taxpayer must pay over 50% of the cost of maintaining a household that is the taxpayer's home. Taxpayer's household must be a dependent relative's principal home.
- Surviving spouse – Married filing jointly rates are applicable for two years after a spouse's death, if the remaining spouse is maintaining a household for a dependent child.

Maintaining a household includes costs such as mortgage interest, home repairs, food consumed on premises, rent, taxes, home insurance, and utilities. These costs do not include expenses for education, clothing, vacations, medical expenses, transportation, and life insurance.

Guidelines for Exemptions

Prior to the TCJA, the Internal Revenue Code allowed a personal exemption for taxpayers and an exemption for the taxpayer's spouse if they file married filing jointly. If the taxpayers filed separate tax returns, a married taxpayer was not permitted to claim an exemption for a spouse unless the spouse did not have any gross income and could not be claimed as another taxpayer's dependent. With the enactment of the TCJA (and particularly with its higher standard deduction), the personal exemption was eliminated.

Dependency Tests

Two dependency tests are:

- Support test – Over 50% of support of the dependent is furnished by the taxpayer. Support may consist of shelter, clothing, food, education, medical and dental expenses, etc. One support test exception is the multiple support agreement, which allows a dependency exemption for a group of taxpayers who supply more than 50% of an individual's support, even though one person does not cover over 50% of the support. Anyone in this group who paid over 10% of the support may claim the exemption, with the written authorization of the remaining group members.
- Gross income test – The exemption amount must be greater than the dependent's gross income. If the alleged dependent has received scholarships, the nontaxable portion, which is for tuition and books, is not included in taxable income. However, the scholarship portion for room and board is included in taxable income. If a parent provides over 50% of support for children who are under age 19 or for children under age 24 who are students, the parent may claim the child as a dependent even if the child's gross income is greater than the exemption amount. For the gross income test, children include natural children, step-children, adopted children, and foster children.

Calculating Taxes and Unearned Income of Children Under Age 19

The following are methods used to calculate taxes and unearned income of children under age 19:

- Tax tables – Taxpayers with income less than $100,000 can use tax tables for tax calculation. Taxable income is calculated by deducting exemptions and deductions from Adjusted Gross Income (AGI) and using the taxpayer's filing status.
- Tax rate schedules – Provides separate schedules of tax percentages for each filing status. Tax rate schedules are often described as statutory, or nominal, rates. The highest rate that is applicable in a taxpayer's tax calculation is the marginal rate. Tax liability divided by taxable income would be the average rate. The United States tax system is based on a graduated, or progressive, tax rate structure, meaning that as the tax base increases, a higher tax rate applies.

Unearned income of children under the age of 19 may be taxed at the same tax rates as for trusts and estates. (Prior to the Tax Cuts & Jobs Act, such income would be taxed at the parent's tax rate, not the tax rate of trusts and estates.) In some cases, the tax applies to children up to age 24. This unearned income includes dividends, taxable interest, rents, pension and annuity income, capital gains, and royalties.

Child and Dependent Care Credit and Foreign Tax Credit

The Child and Dependent Care Credit is a designated percentage of expenses to help a taxpayer either look for a job or work at a current job. This nonrefundable credit applies to employment-related expenses for child and dependent care. Taxpayers may be eligible for this credit if the taxpayer is providing for a household containing either a dependent under the age of 13 or a dependent or spouse who is physically or mentally incapacitated. This credit ranges from 20% to 35% of the amount paid for qualifying dependent care and qualifying household expenses acquired to maintain employment. As of 2023, qualifying expenses can be up to $3,000 for one qualifying individual or $6,000 for more than one qualifying individual. For tax year 2021 only, this was increased to $8,000 and $16,000 respectively due to the American Rescue Plan Act (ARPA), and the maximum credit increased to 50% (from 35%).

Taxpayers are allowed a tax credit for foreign income tax paid on income earned and taxed in another country. The foreign tax credit works as an offset against the tax liability to prevent taxpayers facing double taxation on income that is taxed by the U.S. and foreign countries. This credit has the following restriction: [{foreign-source taxable income/(exemptions+ taxable income)} * U.S. tax prior to FTC]. Passive income is subject to a separate computation for the FTC restriction. If foreign taxes are used as a deduction, the above restriction is not applicable. If the FTC is greater than the total restriction, the FTC credit may be carried back one year and carried forward 10 years.

Child Tax Credit

The Child Tax Credit is based on the taxpayer's number of eligible dependent children. For 2023, the maximum child tax credit is $2,000 per qualifying child; a qualifying child is under age 17, the taxpayer's dependent, and a U.S. citizen. Additionally, there is a $500 family credit for other dependents like aging parents. The AGI phase-out ranges for the child tax credit start at $400,000 for married filing jointly taxpayers, $200,000 for single taxpayers and heads of households, and $200,000 for married filing separately taxpayers. For every $1,000 exceeding the AGI threshold limits, the credit is reduced by $50.

Credit for Elderly and Disabled Taxpayers

The Credit for Elderly or Disabled Taxpayers is available for taxpayers age 65 and older or for taxpayers under age 65 who have retired due to a permanent complete disability and who receive disability income. It is intended to assist taxpayers who are not receiving significant tax-free retirement benefits. This nonrefundable credit is restricted to the tax liability amount; it is 15% of an initial amount that has had deductions of specific amounts that are not included in gross income. This credit cannot be carried back and cannot be carried forward.

Taxes Withheld and General Business Credit

- Tax withheld – This functions the same as a refundable credit
- General business credit – Nonrefundable credit that combines other credits, such as business energy, work opportunity, research activities, disabled access credit, and low-income housing credit. Unused general business credit may be carried forward 20 years or back 1 year.

Forms W-2, W-3, SS-4, 940, and 941

The Form W-2, Wage and Tax Statement, provides an employee with wages paid, FICA, and income tax withholdings. The Form W-2 must be distributed no later than January 31 for the previous year. This form is used by the employee to file his income tax return and to notify the Social Security Administration (SSA) of the FICA wages earned by the employee. The Form W-3, Transmittal of Wage and Tax Statements is filed by the employer with Forms W-2 to the SSA. It provides totals and reconciliation of FICA withholdings and income tax withholdings reported on Form W-2. The Form SS-4, Application for Employer Identification Number (EIN) is an application for an employer to obtain an EIN to be used on all other forms filed with the SSA and the IRS. The EIN is a 9-digit number hyphenated between the 2nd and 3rd digits (e.g., 72-0123456). The Form 940 or Form 940 EZ, Employer's Annual FUTA Tax Return, must be filed by January 31 for the previous year to notify the federal government with an accounting for Federal Unemployment Tax. The employer must send any undeposited FUTA owed along with the form. The Form 941, Employer's Quarterly Federal Tax Return, must be filed by the last day of the month after the end of each calendar quarter to report quarterly employment taxes.

AMT for Individuals

The Alternative Minimum Tax (AMT) is a separate system from the normal income tax system. For both systems' tax purposes, most income and expense items are handled the same way. Some specific itemized deductions, including charitable contributions, are permitted for both AMT purposes and normal income tax purposes. Salaries are included in both regular taxable income calculations and alternative minimum taxable income (AMTI). Differences between the systems include that personal and dependency exemptions are not permitted for AMT purposes. Municipal bond interest income is not included in the taxable income calculation in the normal tax system. However, if the bonds are private activity bonds, municipal bond interest income is included in AMTI. Some items result in different amounts between the two tax methods. Depreciation may be deducted in both systems, but the depreciation deduction amount can be different. These differences usually result in AMTI differing from normal taxable income. AMT is calculated by multiplying the AMT base by a two-tiered rate schedule. For 2023, a married filing jointly taxpayer's first $220,700 of AMTI over the exemption amount is subject to the 26% rate; the taxpayer's AMTI more than $220,700 over the exemption amount is subject to the 28% rate. There are different thresholds for other filing statuses.

AMT Adjustments

Alternative Minimum Tax (AMT) adjustments for individuals are generally due to differences in timing, which will reverse in subsequent periods, between the AMT system and the normal income tax system. The adjustment amount and direction (positive or negative) of the amount needs to be determined. If the deduction permitted for AMT purposes is greater than the deduction permitted for normal income tax purposes, the difference is a negative adjustment. If the deduction permitted for normal income tax calculations is greater than the deduction permitted for AMT purposes, the difference is a positive adjustment. If the income reported for AMT purposes is greater than the regular income tax income reported, the difference is a positive adjustment. If the regular income tax income reported is greater than the AMT income reported, the difference is a negative adjustment.

AMT adjustments for individuals include the following:

- Regarding depreciation of real property placed in service after 1986 and prior to 1999, the difference between straight-line depreciation and normal tax depreciation over 40 years.

- Regarding personal property put into service after 1986, the difference between normal tax depreciation and 150% declining balance depreciation (changing to straight-line if needed to maximize the deduction).
- AMT does not permit deductions for standard deductions and personal exemptions.
- AMT method does not permit deductions for state, local, property, and foreign income taxes; miscellaneous itemized deductions subject to the AGI 2% floor are not permitted in computing AMT either.
- AMT permits a qualified housing interest deduction instead of qualified residence interest. A qualified housing interest consists only of interest incurred to obtain, build, or significantly improve a taxpayer's primary residence.
- AMT uses a 10% AGI floor in the computation of deductible medical expenses.
- In the AMT tax calculation, the excess of stock value over the exercise price is considered an adjustment in the first taxable year that the stock rights are freely transferable or a substantial forfeiture risk is not applicable. The exercise of incentive stock options does not increase normal taxable income.
- Difference between the completed contract amount reported and the percentage of completion income reported for long-term contracts. AMT method requires the percentage of completion method.

AMT Formula

AMT formula for Individuals:

Normal taxable income

+/- adjustments

= Alternative Minimum Taxable Income (AMTI) Exemption Amount

= AMT base

x 26% or 28% rate

= Tentative tax before foreign tax credit AMT foreign tax credit

= Tentative minimum tax Normal tax liability (less any allowable foreign tax credit)

= AMT (if positive amount)

The AMT formula is intended to reconcile AMTI to taxable income. The reconciliation is done by accounting for differences between the two systems by noting reconciling items, which are called tax preferences (always positive) or AMT adjustments (may be positive or negative).

Exemptions and Credits for AMT Purposes

The exemption amount works in the taxpayer's favor when he does not have many positive adjustments and tax preferences so that he may get out of the burden of AMT. This exemption amount works to offset Alternative Minimum Taxable Income (AMTI). During the phase-out range, the AMT exemption amount is phased out at 25% of AMTI. For tax year 2023, for married filing jointly taxpayers and surviving spouses, the AMT exemption amount is $126,500 and the phase-out threshold is $1,156,300. The AMT exemption for head of household taxpayers and single taxpayers is $81,300, and the phase-out threshold is $578,150. The AMT exemption for married filing separately taxpayers is $63,250, and the phase-out threshold is $578,150. To make things fair for the taxpayer with the reversal of timing differences, a tax credit for prior years' minimum tax liability associated with timing differences may be deducted from the normal income tax liability (not from future AMT liability). The alternative minimum tax credit may be carried forward into future years. The amount of AMT paid is calculated net of exclusion preferences.

AMT Preferences for Individuals

Alternative Minimum Tax (AMT) preferences for individuals are items that are not permitted for purposes of the AMT that were permitted in the normal income tax calculations. These items created tax benefits in the normal income tax calculations. These items include the following:

- Private activity bond interest is used in computing alternative minimum tax income (AMTI). Private activity bonds are state- or municipality-issued bonds with greater than 10% of the proceeds with planned private business use. Expenses associated with the bonds are offset against the interest income in the tax preference calculation. This is not permitted for normal tax calculations.
- The percentage depletion preference is the amount of the excess of the percentage depletion for normal income tax deduction which is greater than the property's adjusted basis at the tax year end.
- Seven percent of the Section 1202 excluded gain on some small business stock excluded gain amount.
- Excess of accelerated depreciation greater than straight-line depreciation for real property and leased personal property put into service prior to 1987.

Home Office Deduction for Self-Employed Taxpayers

In 2013, the IRS introduced a new deduction to anyone who is self-employed. They have the option to claim a new, simplified deduction for a home office. The deduction is calculated as $5/square foot of home office space, up to a maximum of 300 square feet. Taxpayers still have the option to figure their own expenses and then pro-rate them, but this is meant to be a simpler deduction.

American Taxpayer Relief Act of 2012

The American Taxpayer Relief Act of 2012 (ATRA) was passed in response to the fiscal cliff looming in January 2013. As various "Bush tax cuts" were expiring at the end of 2012, ATRA made the expiration of these tax cuts more tolerable for the middle class; i.e. tax rates increased less than otherwise. Specifically, ATRA permanently established the marginal tax rate percentages for most taxpayers (10%, 15%, 25%, 28%, 33%, and 35%), adding a 39.6% tax bracket for high-income earners. These tax brackets are indexed for inflation moving forward.

- ATRA also locked in some tax credits beneficial to middle- and lower-income individuals, the American Opportunity Tax Credit (through 2017), the Earned Income Tax Credit (through 2017), and the Child Tax Credit (permanently).
- Whereas the threshold income for the alternative minimum tax (AMT) was never previously set in stone, ATRA permanently established that threshold income, indexed for inflation.
- Unfortunately, ATRA did not extend the payroll tax "holiday" which had been enjoyed for the previous two years: the employee portion of the FICA taxes increased from 5.65% back to 7.65% of payroll income.
- ATRA increased taxation for the wealthy, not merely by adding the 39.6% rate, but by adding a 20% capital gains tax rate and reducing the deductions and exemptions which high earners could claim.
- Numerous ATRA provisions were modified or undone by the Tax Cuts & Jobs Act.

NIIT

The Net Investment Income Tax (NIIT), more formally termed the Unearned Income Medicare Contribution Surtax, is an additional income tax of 3.8% (as of 2023), beyond the ordinary federal income tax, imposed on a taxpayer's "net investment income," which generally includes income from dividends, rent, interest, royalties, and capital gains. The NIIT was included as part of the Affordable Care Act (Obamacare) in order to fund the provisions of that Act. Strictly speaking, the NIIT does not always apply to one's net investment income, for, to avoid imposition on lower-income earners, the taxable base is calculated as the *lesser* of (i) net investment income or (ii) the excess of one's modified adjusted gross income (MAGI) over a designated threshold. This threshold is $200,000 for single taxpayers and $250,000 for those married filing jointly. (For instance, a MFJ taxpayer with a MAGI of $260,000 and net investment income of $25,000 would pay the 3.8% tax only on $10,000.) Despite being simple on its face, this tax becomes quite complex regarding the definition of "net investment income," generating controversy concerning its applicability to the sale of ownership interests in pass-through entities, income from "self-rentals" to a business one owns, and other such transactions.

Additional Medicare Tax

Two of the new taxes imposed by the Affordable Care Act (Obamacare) to fund the new healthcare system are the "Unearned Income Medicare Contribution Surtax," a.k.a. the Net Investment Income Tax (NIIT), and the Additional Medicare Tax. While the NIIT is imposed on net investment income, the Additional Medicare Tax is imposed on Medicare wages (i.e. wages subject to the Medicare portion of FICA), insofar as such wages surpass a certain threshold. As of 2023, taxpayers with Medicare wages in excess of $200,000 (if single) or $250,000 (if married filing jointly) must pay a further 0.9%, beyond the ordinary Medicare tax of 1.45%, on those excess wages. For example, if a married couple makes $300,000 in Medicare wages during a tax year, they will owe 1.45% on the first $250,000 and 2.35% on the last $50,000, yielding a total Medicare tax liability of $4,800. Note that this Additional Medicare Tax does not apply to the employer. While the employer always must pay his portion of FICA – 1.45% of an employee's net wages *on top of* the total wages he pays to the employee – the employer is not bound to pay the extra 0.9% on excess Medicare wages. He is bound only to *withhold* the 0.9% of an employee's wages from that employee's paycheck, forwarding the amount to the government.

Federal Taxation of Entities

Corporation Reorganizations

Corporation reorganization types:

- Type A: consolidation or statutory merger
- Type B: corporation acquisition of another corporation accomplished completely by the stock of each corporation
- Type C: stock-for-asset exchange between corporations
- Type D: corporation asset transfer to another corporation in which the shareholders of the first corporation are controlling the second corporation upon the asset transfer
- Type E: corporation recapitalization
- Type F: organizational change related to form, identity, or location
- Type G: corporation transfer of assets to another corporation as a result of a receivership or bankruptcy proceeding

There are specific property or stock exchanges in a corporation reorganization that will result in a gain or loss deferral.

Gain Recognition Upon Formation of Partnership

Typically, there is no gain recognition when a partnership is formed. However, there are exceptions under the following circumstances:

- The transaction is a property sale that is disguised. This can happen when a partner will contribute property that is appreciated to the partnership and, shortly after the contribution, the partner will obtain a partnership distribution. This "distribution" could create the appearance of the partnership buying the property from the partner. Additionally, if the partnership assumes the partner's liabilities, the IRS may view this as the partnership buying the partner's property.
- A partner contributes appreciated stocks to an investment partnership. The partner making the contribution may have to recognize any realized gains on the stocks when he makes this contribution.
- The partner exchanges services for an interest in the partnership. Services are not considered to be property and are not transferable to the partnership as a tax-free exchange. In this situation, the partner will recognize normal compensation that is the partnership interest's fair market value.

Corporation Dividends

For corporations, dividends are not usually deductible. For shareholders, dividends may be treated as capital gain, ordinary income, or a nontaxable capital recovery; usually, dividends will be ordinary income to the shareholder. There are several factors to consider for the tax implications of dividends: the property type being distributed, the shareholder's stock basis, whether a liquidating or nonliquidating distribution is taking place, earnings availability, and if the distribution causes the shareholder to surrender any ownership. To calculate the distribution amount, add the cash distribution to the value of any property received less any liabilities that were assumed. Gain will be recognized by the corporation for any appreciated property distributed in the same manner as if the property were sold for its fair market value. Losses are not recognized for property distributions to shareholders if the distributions are nonliquidating. Property distributions result in:

- Dividend as ordinary income, to be included in the shareholder's gross income. These distributions are generally paid from the corporation's Earnings & Profits, either current or accumulated.
- Stock basis return will be deemed to have happened if the corporation does not have enough Earnings & Profits to support the dividend. This portion is not taxable.
- Capital gains will be received by the shareholder if the dividend is not supported by Earnings & Profits and the stock basis.

Proportionate Distributions from Partnerships

Gains or losses are not recognized in a distribution by the partnership. If a distribution includes more than one property item, the partner's basis is decreased in the following order: cash, inventory and unrealized receivables bases, and property adjusted basis. Gains will be recognized by the partner for the amount of cash greater than the basis in the partnership. Loss will only be recognized if the partnership interest is 100% liquidated by the partner acquiring cash, inventory, or unrealized receivables. In a distribution that is nonliquidating, distributed property basis to the partner is typically equal to the previous property basis to the partnership. This distributed property basis is restricted to the partnership interest basis minus any cash received. If a retired or deceased partner's partnership interest is liquidated, the distribution payments cause capital gains or losses to the partner.

Partnership Disproportionate Distributions

A partnership disproportionate distribution happens in the following cases:

- Pertaining to a partner's portion of significantly appreciated inventory or unrealized receivables.
- Gain or loss may be recognized by the partner.
- Gain or loss may be recognized by the partnership in cases of a distribution that is not proportionate relating to inventory that is significantly appreciated or unrealized receivables.

Corporation Stock Liquidations

From a tax standpoint, a corporate liquidation occurs when a corporation ceases to be a going concern. Liquidations may result if the business has a lack of success, if shareholders desire to distribute corporation assets and terminate the corporation, or if another party desires to buy the corporation's assets. When a shareholder receives property in a corporate liquidation, the property basis will be the property's fair market value. When a shareholder receives money in a corporate liquidation, for tax purposes, the money is considered to be received in exchange for stock, creating a capital gain or loss. Typically, a liquidating corporation distributing corporation assets will recognize gain or loss on the sale from the asset distribution. In the liquidation of a subsidiary, neither the parent nor subsidiary has any recognition of gain or loss. To be eligible for this provision, the parent has to own a minimum of 80% of the subsidiary's voting stock and 80% of the subsidiary's total stock. All tax accounting attributes and asset property bases will be transferred to the parent corporation. This nonrecognition of gains and losses is not available to minority shareholders. Typically, liquidating corporations do not recognize losses resulting from property distributions to related parties as long as the property acquisition occurred in the five years prior to the property distribution date or as a capital contribution. In this case, a related party is a shareholder owning the majority of the corporation's stock.

Asset Acquisitions Resulting from Purchase of Stock

If a corporation buys a minimum of 80% of another corporation's stock over the span of twelve months, the stock purchase will be considered an asset acquisition. The corporation associated with the stock that was bought is treated as having sold 100% of its assets on the date of acquisition and to have bought those assets on the day after the date of acquisition.

Partnership Allocations

Partnership Distributions

Income and guaranteed payments distributed to partners are considered to have passed from the partnership to the partner on the last day of the tax year of the partnership.

Sale of Partnership Interest

Partnership interests are considered capital assets that typically result in capital gains or losses when disposed of. The selling and buying partners' outside bases include the partners' proportionate share of partnership debt. The selling and buying partners split partnership income or loss proportionately; the selling partner's basis should be adjusted prior to the computation of the sale gain or loss. Gain is equal to the amount realized that is greater than the partnership interest adjusted basis. If inventory or unrealized receivables exist, the selling partner's total gain or loss is recategorized as a capital gain or loss and an ordinary income or loss pertaining to the inventory or unrealized receivables of the partnership. Unrealized receivables will include any potential § 1245, 1250, and 1252 recapture, as well as the accounts receivable of taxpayers using the cash basis accounting method. Inventory consists of all assets, excluding § 1231 assets, capital assets, and cash.

Corporation Reconciliation of Book Income and Taxable Income

Corporations must complete Schedule M-1 of Form 1120 to reconcile taxable income per the income tax return with the net income from a financial accounting standpoint. Schedule M-1 begins with the financial accounting (book) net income and the following additions are added in:

- Any capital losses greater than capital gains (deductions are not allowed for net capital losses)
- Tax liability for federal income tax
- Income reported during the current taxable year that is not reported for book income purposes, such as prepayments.
- Deductions permitted in computing net income per books but not permitted for taxable income computations, such as charitable contributions greater than the 10% restriction

The following are subtracted from book income:

- Deductions for tax purposes that are not included in book income.
- Income included in book income but not included in income for tax purposes, such as tax-exempt interest.
- Dividends received deduction (DRD).
- To determine book income from taxable income, reverse the above adjustments.
- Schedule M-3 applies to corporations with assets of $10 million or greater. It replaces Schedule M-1.

Schedule M-1 reflects both temporary differences and permanent differences. An example of a permanent difference is the treatment of tax-exempt interest. Tax-exempt interest is always exempt for taxable income and always included in book income. Temporary differences are usually due to timing differences. An example would be prepaid income. Schedule M-2 is used as a reconciliation of unappropriated retained earnings as of the beginning of the taxable year with unappropriated retained earnings as of the end of the taxable year. This reconciliation is done by adding any miscellaneous increases affecting retained earnings to book income and deducting any dividends or other miscellaneous decreases affecting retained earnings. Schedule M-3 applies to corporations with assets of $10 million or greater. It replaces Schedule M-1.

Disclosures Under Schedule M-3

Schedule M-3 shows the difference between financial accounting net income and taxable income for businesses possessing $10 million or more in total assets. It requires a very high level of detail, including full lists of items pertinent to income and expenses. Temporary and permanent differences between financial accounting net income and taxable income also need to be separately reported. Companies using Schedule M-3 must reconcile the total consolidated net income to the net incomes of other corporations included in the entity.

Corporate Tax Filing Guidelines

Corporations are required to file a federal income tax return whether or not they have taxable income. Corporate income tax returns are filed on Form 1120 and are due by the 15th day of the 4th month following the close of the tax year; calendar-year corporate tax returns are due on April 15. Corporations obtain an automatic six-month extension by filing Form 7004 by the return due date. Small corporations are permitted to file a shorter form, Form 1120-A, if each of the following is less than $500,000: total income, total assets, and gross receipts. Corporations pay taxes on earnings as reflected on the tax return. Corporations distribute earnings to the owners (shareholders) in the form of dividends. Shareholders are required to pay taxes on their personal tax returns, which reflect dividend income (double taxation).

C Corporation's Taxable Income or Loss

To calculate the taxable income for a C corporation, one must take the corporation's total revenue (both ordinary/operating and investing revenue), subtract total non-capital business expenses (e.g., wages), calculate total capital business expenses and deduct the depreciable portion of the expenses for the current year in order to obtain the taxable income or loss. The applicable tax rates are then applied to this income or loss, at which point the corporation might also claim some tax credit to reduce their tax obligation.

Corporate and Individual Calculation of Gross Income

Gross income calculations for corporations are similar to gross income calculations for individuals. Corporate gross income includes business income, property gains, rents and royalties, dividends and interest, etc. Corporations and individuals are allowed certain gross income exclusions; corporations are not permitted as many gross income exclusions as individuals. Another common gross income factor is that municipal bond interest is not included in gross income for both corporations and individuals.

Determination of Corporate and Individual Property Gains and Losses

Property gains and losses for corporations are treated in a similar manner to individuals. For both corporations and individuals, capital or ordinary gains and losses are determined by the asset type. Both individuals and corporations do not recognize gain or loss achieved through exchanges of like-kind property; for involuntary conversions, both individuals and corporations may elect to defer gain recognition. The rules governing losses disallowed due to transactions between related parties or wash sales of securities are applicable to both corporations and individuals. Recapture guidelines are applicable to both corporations and individuals.

Corporation Estimated Tax Payments

Corporations are required to pay estimated tax payments unless expected tax liability is less than $500. The estimated tax is calculated by deducting the corporation's allowable tax credits from its anticipated tax liability. Estimated tax payments are due on a quarterly basis – the 15th day of the 4th, 6th, 9th, and 12th month of every tax year. For a calendar-year corporate taxpayer, estimated tax payments are due on 4/15, 6/15, 9/15, and 12/15. No penalty will be assessed for underpayment of estimated tax as long as the payments at a minimum equal the lesser of the prior year's tax or the current year's tax. If based on the prior year, the prior year must have been a complete 12 months and had a tax liability; if based on the current year, tax is evaluated by either actual income or annualized income. Large corporations may use tne prior year's tax as the estimated income tax payment basis for the 1st quarterly installment; remaining quarterly payments must be based on current year tax. If corporations fail to pay taxes amounting to 90% of the total tax owed, there is a penalty assessed of 0.5% per month, up to 25%. If taxes are not paid by the tax return's original due date, interest payments are required from the return's due date until the tax is paid.

AMT for Corporations

Prior to the Tax Cuts & Jobs Act, the corporate AMT was calculated similarly to the individual AMT, involving an exemption threshold and a phaseout of that exemption for higher-income corporations. But the corporate AMT was entirely repealed with the passing of the TCJA.

Deductibility of Business Expenses and Securities Having No Value

Deductions are allowed for all necessary and normal business expenses. This includes expenses for the use of business property, reasonable salary expenses, and 50% of self-employment taxes paid. All of these expenses must be reasonable amounts. These expenses are categorized as deductions for AGI. The following expenses are not permitted to be categorized as business expenses: fines and penalties, charitable contributions, and illegal transactions. Securities with no value can be considered deductible if the security becomes totally worthless during the year. They are considered capital losses that occurred on the last day of the taxable year.

Terms Pertaining to Securities

- Insider: A corporate officer, shareholder, or director owning greater than 10% of a registered security. To compute the percentage, include the aggregate total of the security owner's spouse, minor children, stock held in trust in which the owner is the beneficiary, and relatives living in the same house.
- Security: A financial instrument reflecting ownership, such as a right, debt instrument, or equity instrument. Examples include options, bonds, and stocks.
- Underwriter: An individual involved with the public distribution of securities.
- Prospectus: A document that goes with a new security issue. It provides similar information as the registration statement, the intended use of the funds, such as a listing of officers and directors, and audited financial statements.
- Registration statement: A required statement that must be filed with the SEC. It includes information pertinent to a new securities issue to provide information to potential investors for them to make a knowledgeable decision. It must be submitted to the SEC prior to securities being sold in interstate commerce.
- Proxy: Used by stockholders to transfer voting rights to another party.
- Tender offer: A bid to buy a company's stock at a designated price.

AETs Applicable to Corporations

Accumulated earnings taxes (AETs) were created to keep companies from retaining earnings unrelated to the company's needs. If companies retain earnings beyond reasonable needs, the AET may be assessed. This will often be done to prevent the taxation of shareholders on distributions of dividends. Personal Holding Companies (PHCs) are not subject to the AET. Accumulated earnings are permitted for the greater of the business's reasonable needs or $250,000 less accumulated E&P at the prior year-end. A 15% tax rate is assessed for accumulated taxable income. Dividend distributions can decrease the accumulated taxable income and prevent an AET assessment.

AET is calculated by:

Taxable income + Deduction for NOL

+ Deduction for dividends received

- Net capital loss

- Charitable contributions greater than the 10% restriction

- Federal income taxes

= Adjusted Taxable income

- Consent dividends

- Credit for accumulated earnings

- Payment of dividends during the latter 9.5 months of the tax year & 2.5 months following the tax year

= Accumulated taxable income

x 15% = Accumulated earnings tax

Capital Losses for Corporations

Individuals are permitted a capital loss deduction of up to $3,000; capital losses exceeding the deduction may carry over indefinitely. Corporations are not allowed a capital loss deduction against ordinary income. Capital losses may only be netted with capital gains. Corporations with a net capital loss may carry the net capital loss back three years, beginning with the first year, and capital losses may also be carried forward for five years. If a corporation carries a long-term capital loss either forward or backward, it is treated as a short-term capital loss.

NOL for Corporations

Net operating losses (NOL) of a corporation may not be carried back, but may be carried forward indefinitely, to be used in offsetting taxable income in the years to which it is carried. (Prior to the TCJA, NOLs could be carried back 2 years and carried forward 20 years.) Should a corporation have a net operating loss due to a presidentially declared disaster, small business corporations are allowed to carry back three years. In calculating net operating losses, corporations are permitted to include the dividend received deduction. Corporations are not allowed a net capital loss deduction; corporations do not consider deductions that are nonbusiness in nature.

Treatment of Stock Exchanges in the Same Corporation

Stock and bond exchanges are not considered to be like-kind exchanges. There is no gain or loss recognition for shareholders with common stock exchanges within the same corporation or for preferred stock exchanges in the same corporation. This is applicable for exchanges between the corporation and the shareholder and between shareholders. Nonrecognition exchanges include exchanges of common stock with different rights, such as nonvoting or voting. There is recognition of gain or loss for stock exchanges in the same corporation, so long as preferred stock is exchanged for common stock, or vice versa. A shareholder's exercise of conversion rights is not a taxable event. The basis of securities sold is established by use of the FIFO method.

Sale of Publicly Traded Securities

Any gains or losses occurring due to the sale will be recognized on the transaction date by both accrual- and cash-basis taxpayers. C corporations and individuals are allowed to roll over taxable capital gain from the sale of publicly traded securities during the 60 days after the sale if the sale proceeds are used to buy small business investment company common stock or a partnership interest. The rollover gain will be deducted from the stock or partnership interest basis. The rollover gain is restricted to $250,000 annually for corporations and $50,000 for individual taxpayers. Individuals are restricted to lifetime gain rollover of $500,000; corporations are restricted to a lifetime gain rollover of $1 million.

Corporation Current E&P

Taxable income adjustments to calculate current earnings and profits (E&P) include:

- Adding the following: tax-exempt income, dividends received deduction, accelerated depreciation, etc.
- Deducting the following: excess charitable contributions for the year they were incurred, net capital losses, federal income taxes paid, related-party losses, nondeductible life insurance premiums for key employees, etc.

Accumulated E&P

The accumulated E&P is the combined aggregate of current E&P for all prior years, as calculated on the first day of the year, less any E&P distributions and NOLs. Should appreciated property be distributed, the recognized gain would increase current E&P. Distributions reduce E&P by the money amount, the distributed property's adjusted basis, and the distributing corporation's obligation face amount. These reductions should be altered by the shareholder's assumption of any liabilities or any liability associated with the property distributed.

Corporation Affiliated Groups

Corporation affiliated groups are created when a corporation owns a minimum of 80% of another corporation's stock value (excluding nonvoting preferred stock) and voting power. Affiliated groups may opt to file a consolidated tax return; however, once this election is made, it continues indefinitely. In the consolidated tax return, dividends between the corporations must be eliminated. If the affiliated group chooses to file separate tax returns, the dividends between the corporations are eligible for a deduction for 100% of dividends received. If the companies choose to file a consolidated tax return, benefits include intercompany transaction gain deferral and netting operating and capital losses with earnings and capital gains among the corporations.

S Corporation

S corporations are classified as corporations while nevertheless being taxed only at the shareholder level, not the corporate level. For an S corporation to form, all of its current shareholders and all who owned shares during the taxable year prior to the election date must provide their consent to the corporation's election. S corporations may not have more than 100 shareholders (though family members may be treated as a singular shareholder), and may only have one class of stock, so that all stockholders have a proportionate share for all distributions and liquidations. A company may choose to be an S corporation by making this election during the previous taxable year or by the 15th day of the 3rd month for the tax year it becomes effective. S corporations must use either the calendar year or the same tax year as the majority shareholders. S corporation tax returns (Form 1120S) are due by the 15th day of the third month (March 15th for S corporations using a calendar tax year) after the taxable year-end.

Allocations of S Corporation Income and Losses

S corporation income and loss allocation is calculated by multiplying the following formula:

(S corporation item) * (% of shares owned) * (% of year that the shares were owned) = (item amount to be reported by the shareholder)

This method is referred to as a per-share, per-day basis. This method may not be used if an S corporation converts to a C corporation and the stockholders opt to allocate income and expenses from the company's books. If the majority of stock is sold or exchanged during the termination year of an S corporation, this method does not apply; the income and expenses must be divided using the financial accounting records. S corporations do not produce earnings and profits; all income and expense items cause adjustments to the shareholder's debt and/or stock. If a shareholder dies, he is deemed to be a shareholder on the date of his death. If a shareholder disposes of stock, he is deemed to be a shareholder on the date that he disposed of the stock. Similar to a partnership, S corporation shareholders are required to report both the shareholder's proportionate share of the S corporation's income, losses, deductions, and credits, and the shareholder's proportionate share of the normal business income calculated by the S corporation.

S Corporation Shareholder Stock Basis Adjustments

Shareholder stock basis is increased due to:

- Contributions of capital
- Acquisitions of stock
- Nontaxable income that is separately stated
- Computed income that is not separately stated
- Depletion greater than the property basis

Shareholder stock basis is decreased (but not below zero) due to:

- S corporation distributions for which the shareholder does not report income
- Computed losses that are not separately reported
- Losses and deductions that are separately reported
- Corporation expenses that are not deductible

S corporation guidelines are similar to those for a partnership regarding the order in which the basis is adjusted:

- + income items
- – distributions not included in gross income
- – noncapital items that are not deductible
- – losses and expenses that are deductible

Items Passed Through Separately to Shareholder

S corporation items that are passed through separately to the shareholder to maintain their individual tax attributes include the following: charitable contributions, income from dividends and interest, net long-term capital gains and losses, net short-term capital gains and losses, nontaxable interest, income taxes paid to foreign countries, net income or loss from either real estate or other rental properties, investment interest expense, income from royalties, and § 1231 net gains or losses.

Loss Restrictions for Shareholders

Shareholders are only permitted to deduct S corporation losses up to the amount of the stock basis in addition to any debt basis for debts that the corporation owes to the shareholder. S corporation loss deductions to shareholders cannot be greater than the shareholder's at-risk basis as of the taxable year end. Passive loss restrictions may apply to S corporation losses. Shareholders may deduct passive losses up to the amount of the shareholder's passive income.

S Corporation Distribution

If earnings and profits are available, distributions are deemed to be tax-free to the amount of the Accumulated Adjustments Account (AAA). Any previously taxed income from tax years prior to 1983 can be distributed without any taxes resulting from the distribution. The distribution remaining is considered an ordinary dividend from accumulated earnings and profit (AEP). To the amount of the other adjustments account (OAA), distributions are not taxed. Any remaining amount is applied as a stock basis tax-free reduction. Any leftover is deemed a gain (usually a capital gain) from a stock sale or exchange. If there are not any earnings and profits available, distributions are tax-free to the amount of stock adjusted basis. Any remainder is considered a stock gain (usually a capital gain) from sale or exchange.

S Corporation Property Distribution

For depreciated property, the shareholder assumes the property's fair market value as the basis. Realized loss is not recognized. For appreciated property, the stock of the shareholder is decreased by the property's fair market value (though not below zero). The S corporation will recognize realized gain; the shareholder's stock will be increased by the gain, making the property basis the same amount as the fair market value. Basically, the recognized gain is handled as if the S corporation sold the property at its fair market value.

S Corporation Taxes

S corporations do not usually pay any federal income taxes. Similar to a partnership, the S corporation functions as a pass-through entity. However, S corporations may be required to pay taxes on either excess passive investment income or built-in gain. S corporations are required to pay estimated tax payments for taxes owed due to excess passive investment income tax, built-in gains tax, and investment credit recapture taxes. A C corporation that is converted to an S corporation must pay taxes on the net recognized built-in gain (1) if the gain is recognized during the following 10 years after the C corporation elects to become an S corporation, and (2) if the gain is resulting from asset fair market values being greater than the adjusted basis of the assets as of the S corporation's first taxable year.

Adjustments to Accumulated Adjustments Account

Corporate AAA (Accumulated Adjustments Account) adjustments in an S corporation are as follows:

- Add the following items:
- Nonseparately computed income

- Excluding tax-exempt income, all Schedule K items
- Depletion greater than property basis
- Subtract the following items:
- Excluding distributions, adjustments such as deductions and losses
- Tax-free from AAA distribution amounts

Computation of Passive Investment Income Penalty Tax

(Passive investment income greater than 25% of the year's gross receipts / passive investment income for the tax year)

x net passive investment income for the year

= Excess net passive income (ENPI)This tax will decrease the shareholder's passive investment income portion. Passive investment income includes any stock sale or exchange gains, dividends, and interest.

Built-in Gains Tax Liability Computation

Choose the smaller of taxable income or the built-in gain

- any capital losses or NOLs that have not expired yet from C corporation tax years.

= tax base

* top corporate tax rate

- AMT credit carryovers or carryforwards of business credits resulting from C corporation tax years

= built-in gains tax liability

Criteria for Small Business Corporation

The criteria for a small business corporation are as follows:

- Domestic corporation (organized and incorporated in the USA)
- Issues only one stock class
- After 2004, the number of shareholders is restricted to 100; from 1998-2004, the restriction was 75 shareholders.
- No nonresident alien shareholders
- Shareholders must be estates, specific trusts, and individuals.
- May own any percentage of a C corporation's stock, as well as all of a qualified subchapter S subsidiary's stock.

LLC

A limited liability company (LLC) is similar to a corporation in that it provides limited personal liability. An LLC incorporates the limited liability feature of corporations with the tax benefits of a partnership. Owners in an LLC are referred to as "members." Members may be other corporations. The members will usually manage the LLC. Members may decide how they wish to divide profits and losses. Members may also decide if they wish for the LLC to be taxed as a corporation or as a flow-through entity (such as a partnership). In an LLC, the members' personal assets are not available to satisfy the debts of the LLC.

Partnerships

A partnership is a business organization established between at least two people to begin a business where each person makes contributions of capital and/or services with the expectation of a share in profits and losses. Partnerships are flow-through entities, meaning profits and losses flow through to the partners; partnerships are not taxed. In a partnership, general partners have unlimited liability. Should a partner desire to sell his interest in the partnership, the other partners must approve the sale. Should a partner withdraw from the partnership or die, the current partnership may end or the partnership may face challenges financially. In a general partnership, all owners may participate in any partnership decisions, creating a decentralized management. Limited partnerships may have centralized management, which has proved to be more effective in business operations.

Tax Reporting

Partnership activities tax reporting:

- The ordinary income of a partnership is reported at the partnership level on Form 1065 page 1 and on page 3, Schedule K, of Form 1065. At the partner level, ordinary income is reported on Schedule K-1. The partner's share of ordinary income is passed through to the partner for separate reporting, and the partner's basis is also increased accordingly.
- The ordinary loss of a partnership is reported at the partnership level on Form 1065 page 1 and on page 3, Schedule K, of Form 1065. At the partner level, the loss is passed through to the partner on Schedule K-1, and the partner's basis is decreased accordingly. Nondeductible losses may be carried forward to future tax years. Partner loss deductions may be restricted.
- Self-employment net income is reported at the partnership level on Form 1065 Schedule K and is reported at the partner level on Schedule K-1.
- Items reported separately are reported on Form 1065 Schedule K at the partnership level and reported on Schedule K-1 at the partner level. The partners' share of each item is passed through separately.

Partnership Ordinary Income

Partnership ordinary income and deductions are combined at the partnership level. These items include the following:

- Income from sales (minus cost of goods sold)
- Expenses including salaries and wages, payroll taxes, supplies, repairs, rents, and bad debts.
- Depreciation
- Recapture for § 1245 and 1250
- Amortization for at least 15 years for business start-up expenses
- Partner guaranteed payments
- Partnerships are not permitted any deduction for standard deductions, personal or dependency exemptions, net operating losses, dividends received, and depletion of oil and gas interests.

Determination of Partnership Tax Year

These guidelines are meant to be followed in order to determine the taxable year:

- The partnership should have the same tax year as the majority partners, those owning over 50% of profits and capital combined.
- If the majority partners do not have the same tax year end, the partnership must have the tax year of the principal partners. Principal partners are partners who own at least 5% of capital or profits from the partnership. In this case, all principal partners are required to have the same tax year.
- If the principal partners do not have the same tax year, the partnership should use the tax year that causes the least aggregate deferred income to partners.

If the partnership does not wish to use the tax year as determined by the above guidelines, the partnership may adopt a different tax year if the partnership can prove a valid business purpose and can obtain permission from the IRS. The partnership can easily prove a valid business purpose if at least 25% of the gross receipts from the partnership have been recognized during the last 2 months of the same 12-month period for three consecutive years. Partnerships have the choice of establishing a new tax year if the year in which the election is made does not end with a deferral period greater than 3 months.

Calculation of Partnership Income

Some partnership income and expenses are netted at the entity level. Other income and expenses must remain distinctive and reported separately on both the partnership tax return and every partner's Schedule K-1. These items are kept separate because there are unique tax attributes applicable to these items.

Items that must be passed through separately include the following:

- Charitable contributions
- Capital gains and losses (both short-term and long-term)
- Deduction for § 179 expenses
- § 1231 gains and losses
- Income from royalties, dividends, and interest
- Taxes paid to foreign countries
- Passive activity items (for example, income or loss from rental real estate)

Partnership Basis

Partner basis calculation:

Original basis

+ Income items allocated to the partner

- Partnership distributions

- Losses and deductions

= Partner adjusted basis

A partnership basis is increased for the following items:

- The proportionate share for the partner of any partnership liability increases.
- The proportionate share for the partner of any partnership income; this includes tax-exempt income and capital gains.
- Adjusted basis for subsequent contributions to capital
- Individual partner liability increase due to a partner assuming a liability of the partnership. This is deemed a capital contribution.

A partnership basis is decreased for the following items:

- Proportionate share for the partner of any partnership deductions and losses (this includes capital losses).
- Proportionate share for the partner of any partnership liability decreases.
- Proportionate share for the partner of any expenses that are not deductible.
- Any money or property (adjusted basis) that the partnership distributes to the partner.
- Individual partner liability decrease due to the partnership assuming the liability. This is deemed a partnership distribution to the partner.
- A partner's basis can never be reduced below zero.

Section 754 Elections

A partnership can elect to adjust the basis of its property if a specific written statement is filed along with the annual report for the partnership for the year in which the property transfer occurs. This written statement needs to include the partnership's name and address, a declaration stating that the partnership elects, according to section 754, to apply the provisions under sections 734(b) and 743(b), and a signature from at least one partner.

Treatment of Transactions Between a Partnership and a Partner

Partnerships and partners may have transactions between them. For example, partners may participate in the following transactions in the capacity of a nonpartner: rentals, property sales, property exchanges, loans, etc. Income resulting from a sale between related parties is considered ordinary income if the property is not a capital asset to either party. Partners and partnerships are not permitted to deduct losses resulting from a related party transaction between them if the partner (related party) owns over 50% of capital or profits in the partnership. Partnership payments to partners may be considered guaranteed payments if the payment is for use of the partner's capital or services and is not derived from partnership income. The partnership may deduct guaranteed payments, and the partner's income will include guaranteed payments. Partner payments may be treated as payments to outside parties. These payments may be deducted if they are for regular business expenses.

Treatment of Partnership Liabilities

Since general partnerships involve the unlimited liability of the partners, the partners' assets are generally able to be claimed by creditors, including for infractions committed by other partners (such as torts or contractual violations related to the partnership's ordinary operations). Yet, if a partnership gains a new partner, he is ordinarily not responsible for the prior infractions committed by other partners. If a partner is departing from a partnership, he will still be liable for the liabilities of other partners until he gives a notice of dissociation to the creditor, or otherwise 90 days after he issues a notice of dissociation.

PARTNERSHIP DISTRIBUTIONS AND SELLING PARTNERSHIP INTEREST

Income and guaranteed payments distributed to partners are considered to have passed from the partnership to the partner on the last day of the tax year of the partnership. Partnership interests are considered capital assets that typically result in capital gains or losses when disposed of. The selling and buying partners' outside bases include the partners' proportionate share of partnership debt. The selling and buying partners split partnership income or loss proportionately; the selling partner's basis should be adjusted prior to the computation of the sale gain or loss. Gain is equal to the amount realized that is greater than the partnership interest adjusted basis. If inventory or unrealized receivables exist, the selling partner's total gain or loss is recategorized as a capital gain or loss and an ordinary income or loss pertaining to the inventory or unrealized receivables of the partnership. Unrealized receivables will include any potential § 1245, 1250, and 1252 recapture, as well as the accounts receivable of taxpayers using the cash basis accounting method. Inventory consists of all assets, excluding § 1231 assets, capital assets, and cash.

FAMILY PARTNERSHIPS AND PARTNERSHIP TERMINATION

Special rules apply, since family partnerships could be used to avoid taxes. In service oriented family partnerships, family members are partners only if the family members have an active role in either performing the services that are needed or in management of the partnership. If the family partnership business income is primarily composed of commissions, fees, or personal service compensation, capital is not considered to be a significant income-producing item. If capital is considered a significant income-producing item, if a family member owns a capital interest in the family partnership business, the family is considered to be a partner.

A partnership is terminated upon the occurrence of either of the following:

- There are no longer two partners.
- During a 12-month period, at least 50% of the capital and profits of the partnership are sold or exchanged.

TRUSTS

A trust is a relationship between two people, the trustee and the beneficiary, in which the trustee has a legal claim to some property in order to better the beneficiary. The trustee can be said to have legal ownership while the beneficiary nonetheless retains equitable ownership. For some relationship to count as a trust, four conditions must obtain. First, there must be a settlor, or trustor, who brings the trust into existence. The settlor can be the trustee or the beneficiary, but cannot be both if there is only one of each. Despite creating the trust, the settlor may or may not have the authority to end it, depending upon what is granted to him according to the terms of the trust. Second, there must be a trustee who has legal title to the property. Third, there must be trust property (or *trust res*), held by the trustee. And fourth, there must be a beneficiary.

Trusts can be living or testamentary, which specify whether the trust becomes effective during or after the grantor's lifetime. A living trust can also be called an "inter-vivos trust." Trusts can also be revocable or irrevocable, which refers to whether the grantor reserves the right to revoke the trust after it becomes effective, including any modifications he might make to the trust's details. (Obviously, then, this distinction applies only to living trusts.) Besides these distinctions, trusts are generally classified by their purpose. For instance, there are asset protection trusts, credit shelter trusts, charitable trusts, dynasty trusts, life insurance trusts, special needs trusts, and many others.

Income Taxes for Estates and Trusts

While estates and nongrantor trusts (i.e., trusts which are not initiated by the trust's grantor) are required to file income taxes as individuals must do, there are some differences. For example, estate and trusts will be taxed at a different rate depending upon whether the income is seen as part of the principal or as part of the distributable net income (DNI) and depending upon whether the income is passed on to the beneficiary. When beneficiaries receive income payments from trusts or estates, such payments can carry tax consequences both for the trust or estate and for the beneficiary. The trust or estate can get a deduction, and beneficiaries are required to report the deduction from Form 1040 as part of their submitted Form 1041. A beneficiary's distributable net income is determined by starting with the trust's or estate's taxable income, excluding the distribution deduction, excluding the personal exemption, excluding the capital gains and losses (since they are generally allocated to principal, not to income), and including tax-exempt interest income.

DNI

Distributable net income (DNI) is the income which is earned by a trust after the expenses have been considered and which can be given to the beneficiary. DNI is relevant in the context of income tax for trusts and estates, as the beneficiary pays taxes on the income as part of his personal income tax. The DNI dictates the amount of distribution deduction for the trust or estate.

Tax Implications of Coverdell Education Savings Plans and SEP Plans

Distributions for qualified higher education expenses receive favorable tax treatment. If Coverdell ESA withdrawals are withdrawn for the payment of the qualified higher education expenses of the designated beneficiary, the Coverdell ESA withdrawals are not taxed. Coverdell ESA contributions are not deductible; taxpayers may contribute up to $2,000 per beneficiary. Qualified higher education expenses are composed of books, uniforms, tuition, room and board, transportation, fees, computers and school supplies. If a taxpayer withdraws a Coverdell ESA distribution that exceeds the qualified higher education expenses, the excess is subject to a 10% penalty and included in the gross income of the distributee. Coverdell ESAs that have not been used by the beneficiary's 30th birthday may be rolled into the Coverdell ESA of another family member without causing any penalties or taxes. Phase-out rules apply for taxpayers within a specific modified AGI range. Taxpayers are permitted to take advantage of the Coverdell ESA provisions and education credits in the same tax year

Simplified Employee Pension (SEP) plans – For tax year 2023, employers are permitted to deduct IRA contributions for employees' accounts the lesser of $66,000 or 25% of the employee's earned income. The compensation limit is capped at $330,000.

REIT

A real estate investment trust (REIT) is a company which owns and operates real estate (or assets related to real estate) for the generation of income. Investors can benefit from this income by investing in such a trust, thereby avoiding the enormous capital investment that would be necessary if they were to purchase the real estate themselves. Examples of real estate owned under a REIT would be office buildings, shopping malls, apartments, hotels, resorts, storage facilities, and warehouses.

QTP

A qualified tuition program (QTP), also known as a 529 plan, is a program which a state (or state agency) implements and maintains for the funding of a student's tuition at an institution of higher education. The program allows facilitates the contribution or prepayments of funds to be used later for a student's higher-education expenses.

TAX-EXEMPT STATUS

In order to be a tax-exempt organization, the organization must meet certain qualifications, apply for tax-exempt status, and then not engage in any outlawed transactions. Application for tax-exempt status requires an official IRS form, though an organization can simply send a written statement if no IRS form is provided for it within fifteen months from the end of the month in which the organization began. Any granting of tax-exempt status applies retroactively to the point in time when the organization came into existence, although any such forms filed late will cause the organization to be exempt from taxation only at the point at which the form is filed. Moreover, while the granting of tax-exempt status ordinarily has retroactive application, the revocation of such a status does too. Private foundations are listed as one of entities qualifying for tax-exempt status. They are any tax-exempt entities other than public charities, usually receiving under one third of their annual funding from members and the public at large. Private foundations are required to comply with further statutory constraints to retain their status. Many tax-exempt organizations must file an annual return identifying their contributions unless they have under $25,000 in gross receipts, or unless they are qualifying religious organizations (or otherwise qualifying organizations as specified by an act of Congress). Private organizations are required to file an annual return regardless of income.

The Internal Revenue Code (IRC) lists the different types of organizations which can qualify as tax-exempt. These include corporations which are established by an act of Congress specifying such a status; corporations or community funds or foundations which are committed to religious, scientific, charitable, public safety, educational, or literary objectives, as well as ones which promote amateur sports competition and prevent cruelty to animals; any business leagues, civic leagues, chambers of commerce, real estate boards, boards of trade, labor organizations, or even professional football leagues that are nonprofit; a club solely for social or recreational purposes which operates only by members' fees, dues, and assessments; employee pension and profit-sharing trusts; private foundations; and some qualifying condominium management associations. Organizations which are created to influence legislation and which are effectively operating for profit (even if they donate all profits to tax-exempt entities) do not qualify for tax-exempt status. Neither do entities promoting amateur sports competition if they also provide athletic equipment and facilities.

UBTI

Unrelated business taxable income (UBTI) is income on which a tax-exempt organization is nevertheless required to pay taxes. The applicable tax rate depends upon whether the entity will be treated as a corporation or as a trust according to IRC § 511(a) and 511(b). The income which is subject to this tax must arise from a trade or business that is regularly carried on by the organization but not significantly related to the organization's tax-exempting purpose.

TCJA

The Tax Cuts & Jobs Act (TCJA) was passed in December 2017. It was the most sweeping piece of tax legislation enacted in decades, accomplishing the following:

- It lowered the individual income tax rates, retaining seven brackets but reducing the higher from 39.6% to 37%.
- It doubled the standard deduction and the child tax credit, although it eliminated personal exemptions.
- It eliminated the domestic products activities deduction (Sec. 199) in favor of the qualified business income deduction (Sec. 199A).
- It doubled the estate tax exemption.

- It reduced the corporate tax rate to a flat 21% (previously a high of 35%).
- It effectively repealed Obamacare's individual mandate penalty by reducing it to $0.
- It eliminated the corporate alternative minimum tax (AMT).
- It moved from a worldwide to a territorial tax system.

How to Overcome Test Anxiety

Just the thought of taking a test is enough to make most people a little nervous. A test is an important event that can have a long-term impact on your future, so it's important to take it seriously and it's natural to feel anxious about performing well. But just because anxiety is normal, that doesn't mean that it's helpful in test taking, or that you should simply accept it as part of your life. Anxiety can have a variety of effects. These effects can be mild, like making you feel slightly nervous, or severe, like blocking your ability to focus or remember even a simple detail.

If you experience test anxiety—whether severe or mild—it's important to know how to beat it. To discover this, first you need to understand what causes test anxiety.

Causes of Test Anxiety

While we often think of anxiety as an uncontrollable emotional state, it can actually be caused by simple, practical things. One of the most common causes of test anxiety is that a person does not feel adequately prepared for their test. This feeling can be the result of many different issues such as poor study habits or lack of organization, but the most common culprit is time management. Starting to study too late, failing to organize your study time to cover all of the material, or being distracted while you study will mean that you're not well prepared for the test. This may lead to cramming the night before, which will cause you to be physically and mentally exhausted for the test. Poor time management also contributes to feelings of stress, fear, and hopelessness as you realize you are not well prepared but don't know what to do about it.

Other times, test anxiety is not related to your preparation for the test but comes from unresolved fear. This may be a past failure on a test, or poor performance on tests in general. It may come from comparing yourself to others who seem to be performing better or from the stress of living up to expectations. Anxiety may be driven by fears of the future—how failure on this test would affect your educational and career goals. These fears are often completely irrational, but they can still negatively impact your test performance.

Elements of Test Anxiety

As mentioned earlier, test anxiety is considered to be an emotional state, but it has physical and mental components as well. Sometimes you may not even realize that you are suffering from test anxiety until you notice the physical symptoms. These can include trembling hands, rapid heartbeat, sweating, nausea, and tense muscles. Extreme anxiety may lead to fainting or vomiting. Obviously, any of these symptoms can have a negative impact on testing. It is important to recognize them as soon as they begin to occur so that you can address the problem before it damages your performance.

The mental components of test anxiety include trouble focusing and inability to remember learned information. During a test, your mind is on high alert, which can help you recall information and stay focused for an extended period of time. However, anxiety interferes with your mind's natural processes, causing you to blank out, even on the questions you know well. The strain of testing during anxiety makes it difficult to stay focused, especially on a test that may take several hours. Extreme anxiety can take a huge mental toll, making it difficult not only to recall test information but even to understand the test questions or pull your thoughts together.

Effects of Test Anxiety

Test anxiety is like a disease—if left untreated, it will get progressively worse. Anxiety leads to poor performance, and this reinforces the feelings of fear and failure, which in turn lead to poor performances on subsequent tests. It can grow from a mild nervousness to a crippling condition. If allowed to progress, test anxiety can have a big impact on your schooling, and consequently on your future.

Test anxiety can spread to other parts of your life. Anxiety on tests can become anxiety in any stressful situation, and blanking on a test can turn into panicking in a job situation. But fortunately, you don't have to let anxiety rule your testing and determine your grades. There are a number of relatively simple steps you can take to move past anxiety and function normally on a test and in the rest of life.

Physical Steps for Beating Test Anxiety

While test anxiety is a serious problem, the good news is that it can be overcome. It doesn't have to control your ability to think and remember information. While it may take time, you can begin taking steps today to beat anxiety.

Just as your first hint that you may be struggling with anxiety comes from the physical symptoms, the first step to treating it is also physical. Rest is crucial for having a clear, strong mind. If you are tired, it is much easier to give in to anxiety. But if you establish good sleep habits, your body and mind will be ready to perform optimally, without the strain of exhaustion. Additionally, sleeping well helps you to retain information better, so you're more likely to recall the answers when you see the test questions.

Getting good sleep means more than going to bed on time. It's important to allow your brain time to relax. Take study breaks from time to time so it doesn't get overworked, and don't study right before bed. Take time to rest your mind before trying to rest your body, or you may find it difficult to fall asleep.

Along with sleep, other aspects of physical health are important in preparing for a test. Good nutrition is vital for good brain function. Sugary foods and drinks may give a burst of energy but this burst is followed by a crash, both physically and emotionally. Instead, fuel your body with protein and vitamin-rich foods.

Also, drink plenty of water. Dehydration can lead to headaches and exhaustion, especially if your brain is already under stress from the rigors of the test. Particularly if your test is a long one, drink water during the breaks. And if possible, take an energy-boosting snack to eat between sections.

Along with sleep and diet, a third important part of physical health is exercise. Maintaining a steady workout schedule is helpful, but even taking 5-minute study breaks to walk can help get your blood pumping faster and clear your head. Exercise also releases endorphins, which contribute to a positive feeling and can help combat test anxiety.

When you nurture your physical health, you are also contributing to your mental health. If your body is healthy, your mind is much more likely to be healthy as well. So take time to rest, nourish your body with healthy food and water, and get moving as much as possible. Taking these physical steps will make you stronger and more able to take the mental steps necessary to overcome test anxiety.

Mental Steps for Beating Test Anxiety

Working on the mental side of test anxiety can be more challenging, but as with the physical side, there are clear steps you can take to overcome it. As mentioned earlier, test anxiety often stems from lack of preparation, so the obvious solution is to prepare for the test. Effective studying may be the most important weapon you have for beating test anxiety, but you can and should employ several other mental tools to combat fear.

First, boost your confidence by reminding yourself of past success—tests or projects that you aced. If you're putting as much effort into preparing for this test as you did for those, there's no reason you should expect to fail here. Work hard to prepare; then trust your preparation.

Second, surround yourself with encouraging people. It can be helpful to find a study group, but be sure that the people you're around will encourage a positive attitude. If you spend time with others who are anxious or cynical, this will only contribute to your own anxiety. Look for others who are motivated to study hard from a desire to succeed, not from a fear of failure.

Third, reward yourself. A test is physically and mentally tiring, even without anxiety, and it can be helpful to have something to look forward to. Plan an activity following the test, regardless of the outcome, such as going to a movie or getting ice cream.

When you are taking the test, if you find yourself beginning to feel anxious, remind yourself that you know the material. Visualize successfully completing the test. Then take a few deep, relaxing breaths and return to it. Work through the questions carefully but with confidence, knowing that you are capable of succeeding.

Developing a healthy mental approach to test taking will also aid in other areas of life. Test anxiety affects more than just the actual test—it can be damaging to your mental health and even contribute to depression. It's important to beat test anxiety before it becomes a problem for more than testing.

Study Strategy

Being prepared for the test is necessary to combat anxiety, but what does being prepared look like? You may study for hours on end and still not feel prepared. What you need is a strategy for test prep. The next few pages outline our recommended steps to help you plan out and conquer the challenge of preparation.

Step 1: Scope Out the Test

Learn everything you can about the format (multiple choice, essay, etc.) and what will be on the test. Gather any study materials, course outlines, or sample exams that may be available. Not only will this help you to prepare, but knowing what to expect can help to alleviate test anxiety.

Step 2: Map Out the Material

Look through the textbook or study guide and make note of how many chapters or sections it has. Then divide these over the time you have. For example, if a book has 15 chapters and you have five days to study, you need to cover three chapters each day. Even better, if you have the time, leave an extra day at the end for overall review after you have gone through the material in depth.

If time is limited, you may need to prioritize the material. Look through it and make note of which sections you think you already have a good grasp on, and which need review. While you are studying, skim quickly through the familiar sections and take more time on the challenging parts.

Write out your plan so you don't get lost as you go. Having a written plan also helps you feel more in control of the study, so anxiety is less likely to arise from feeling overwhelmed at the amount to cover.

Step 3: Gather Your Tools

Decide what study method works best for you. Do you prefer to highlight in the book as you study and then go back over the highlighted portions? Or do you type out notes of the important information? Or is it helpful to make flashcards that you can carry with you? Assemble the pens, index cards, highlighters, post-it notes, and any other materials you may need so you won't be distracted by getting up to find things while you study.

If you're having a hard time retaining the information or organizing your notes, experiment with different methods. For example, try color-coding by subject with colored pens, highlighters, or post-it notes. If you learn better by hearing, try recording yourself reading your notes so you can listen while in the car, working out, or simply sitting at your desk. Ask a friend to quiz you from your flashcards, or try teaching someone the material to solidify it in your mind.

Step 4: Create Your Environment

It's important to avoid distractions while you study. This includes both the obvious distractions like visitors and the subtle distractions like an uncomfortable chair (or a too-comfortable couch that makes you want to fall asleep). Set up the best study environment possible: good lighting and a comfortable work area. If background music helps you focus, you may want to turn it on, but otherwise keep the room quiet. If you are using a computer to take notes, be sure you don't have any other windows open, especially applications like social media, games, or anything else that could distract you. Silence your phone and turn off notifications. Be sure to keep water close by so you stay hydrated while you study (but avoid unhealthy drinks and snacks).

Also, take into account the best time of day to study. Are you freshest first thing in the morning? Try to set aside some time then to work through the material. Is your mind clearer in the afternoon or evening? Schedule your study session then. Another method is to study at the same time of day that you will take the test, so that your brain gets used to working on the material at that time and will be ready to focus at test time.

Step 5: Study!

Once you have done all the study preparation, it's time to settle into the actual studying. Sit down, take a few moments to settle your mind so you can focus, and begin to follow your study plan. Don't give in to distractions or let yourself procrastinate. This is your time to prepare so you'll be ready to fearlessly approach the test. Make the most of the time and stay focused.

Of course, you don't want to burn out. If you study too long you may find that you're not retaining the information very well. Take regular study breaks. For example, taking five minutes out of every hour to walk briskly, breathing deeply and swinging your arms, can help your mind stay fresh.

As you get to the end of each chapter or section, it's a good idea to do a quick review. Remind yourself of what you learned and work on any difficult parts. When you feel that you've mastered the material, move on to the next part. At the end of your study session, briefly skim through your notes again.

But while review is helpful, cramming last minute is NOT. If at all possible, work ahead so that you won't need to fit all your study into the last day. Cramming overloads your brain with more information than it can process and retain, and your tired mind may struggle to recall even previously learned information when it is overwhelmed with last-minute study. Also, the urgent nature of cramming and the stress placed on your brain contribute to anxiety. You'll be more likely to go to the test feeling unprepared and having trouble thinking clearly.

So don't cram, and don't stay up late before the test, even just to review your notes at a leisurely pace. Your brain needs rest more than it needs to go over the information again. In fact, plan to finish your studies by noon or early afternoon the day before the test. Give your brain the rest of the day to relax or focus on other things, and get a good night's sleep. Then you will be fresh for the test and better able to recall what you've studied.

Step 6: Take a Practice Test

Many courses offer sample tests, either online or in the study materials. This is an excellent resource to check whether you have mastered the material, as well as to prepare for the test format and environment.

Check the test format ahead of time: the number of questions, the type (multiple choice, free response, etc.), and the time limit. Then create a plan for working through them. For example, if you have 30 minutes to take a 60-question test, your limit is 30 seconds per question. Spend less time on the questions you know well so that you can take more time on the difficult ones.

If you have time to take several practice tests, take the first one open book, with no time limit. Work through the questions at your own pace and make sure you fully understand them. Gradually work up to taking a test under test conditions: sit at a desk with all study materials put away and set a timer. Pace yourself to make sure you finish the test with time to spare and go back to check your answers if you have time.

After each test, check your answers. On the questions you missed, be sure you understand why you missed them. Did you misread the question (tests can use tricky wording)? Did you forget the information? Or was it something you hadn't learned? Go back and study any shaky areas that the practice tests reveal.

Taking these tests not only helps with your grade, but also aids in combating test anxiety. If you're already used to the test conditions, you're less likely to worry about it, and working through tests until you're scoring well gives you a confidence boost. Go through the practice tests until you feel comfortable, and then you can go into the test knowing that you're ready for it.

Test Tips

On test day, you should be confident, knowing that you've prepared well and are ready to answer the questions. But aside from preparation, there are several test day strategies you can employ to maximize your performance.

First, as stated before, get a good night's sleep the night before the test (and for several nights before that, if possible). Go into the test with a fresh, alert mind rather than staying up late to study.

Try not to change too much about your normal routine on the day of the test. It's important to eat a nutritious breakfast, but if you normally don't eat breakfast at all, consider eating just a protein bar. If you're a coffee drinker, go ahead and have your normal coffee. Just make sure you time it so that the caffeine doesn't wear off right in the middle of your test. Avoid sugary beverages, and drink enough water to stay hydrated but not so much that you need a restroom break 10 minutes into the test. If your test isn't first thing in the morning, consider going for a walk or doing a light workout before the test to get your blood flowing.

Allow yourself enough time to get ready, and leave for the test with plenty of time to spare so you won't have the anxiety of scrambling to arrive in time. Another reason to be early is to select a good seat. It's helpful to sit away from doors and windows, which can be distracting. Find a good seat, get out your supplies, and settle your mind before the test begins.

When the test begins, start by going over the instructions carefully, even if you already know what to expect. Make sure you avoid any careless mistakes by following the directions.

Then begin working through the questions, pacing yourself as you've practiced. If you're not sure on an answer, don't spend too much time on it, and don't let it shake your confidence. Either skip it and come back later, or eliminate as many wrong answers as possible and guess among the remaining ones. Don't dwell on these questions as you continue—put them out of your mind and focus on what lies ahead.

Be sure to read all of the answer choices, even if you're sure the first one is the right answer. Sometimes you'll find a better one if you keep reading. But don't second-guess yourself if you do immediately know the answer. Your gut instinct is usually right. Don't let test anxiety rob you of the information you know.

If you have time at the end of the test (and if the test format allows), go back and review your answers. Be cautious about changing any, since your first instinct tends to be correct, but make sure you didn't misread any of the questions or accidentally mark the wrong answer choice. Look over any you skipped and make an educated guess.

At the end, leave the test feeling confident. You've done your best, so don't waste time worrying about your performance or wishing you could change anything. Instead, celebrate the successful completion of this test. And finally, use this test to learn how to deal with anxiety even better next time.

Review Video: Test Anxiety
Visit mometrix.com/academy and enter code: 100340

Important Qualification

Not all anxiety is created equal. If your test anxiety is causing major issues in your life beyond the classroom or testing center, or if you are experiencing troubling physical symptoms related to your anxiety, it may be a sign of a serious physiological or psychological condition. If this sounds like your situation, we strongly encourage you to seek professional help.

Online Resources

Due to our efforts to try to keep this book to a manageable length, we've created a link that will give you access to all of your online resources:

mometrix.com/resources719/cparegulation

It's Your Moment, Let's Celebrate It!

Share your story @mometrixtestpreparation